KEY IDEAS IN COMMERCIAL LAW

This book unpacks the themes and controversies that pervade commercial law. Commercial parties trade in three things: property, services and credit. In all but the most basic of businesses, a commercial enterprise must have more than one individual empowered to transact on its behalf.

The rules at the heart of commercial law are those that govern when and how a person can bargain for property, services and credit, and to acquire, dispose of, and create interests in assets. Many of these are default rules, which the parties can vary by agreement. Other rules – such as those concerning the priority of competing title claims to assets – are mandatory. Commercial law also involves the taking and allocation of two types of risk: the risk of inadequate or non-performance of agreed obligations, and the risk that counterparties will lack the means to pay what is owed.

This book explores the key ideas in commercial law through these five topics: trade, transacting, title, performance risk, and credit risk.

Key Ideas in Law: Volume 5

Key Ideas in Law

Series Editor: Nicholas J McBride

Hart Publishing's series *Key Ideas in Law* offers short, stimulating introductions to legal subjects, providing an opportunity to step back from the detail of the law to consider its broader intellectual foundations and ideas, and how these work in practice.

Written by leading legal scholars with great expertise and depth of knowledge, these books offer an unparalleled combination of accessibility, concision, intellectual breadth and originality in legal writing.

Each volume will appeal to students seeking a concise introduction to a subject, stimulating wider reading for a course or deeper understanding for an exam, as well as to scholars and practitioners for the fresh perspectives and new ideas they provide.

Recent titles in this series:

**For the complete list of titles in this series,
see www.bloomsbury.com/uk/series/key-ideas-in-law/**

Key Ideas in
Commercial Law

William Day

·HART·

OXFORD · LONDON · NEW YORK · NEW DELHI · SYDNEY

HART PUBLISHING

Bloomsbury Publishing Plc

Kemp House, Chawley Park, Cumnor Hill, Oxford, OX2 9PH, UK

1385 Broadway, New York, NY 10018, USA

29 Earlsfort Terrace, Dublin 2, Ireland

HART PUBLISHING, the Hart/Stag logo, BLOOMSBURY and the Diana logo are
trademarks of Bloomsbury Publishing Plc

First published in Great Britain 2023

Copyright © William Day, 2023

William Day has asserted his right under the Copyright, Designs and Patents
Act 1988 to be identified as Author of this work.

A catalogue record for this book is available from the British Library.

A catalogue record for this book is available from the Library of Congress.

Library of Congress Control Number: 2023934436

ISBN: PB: 978-150994-422-4
       ePDF: 978-150994-424-8
       ePub: 978-150994-423-1

Typeset by Compuscript Ltd, Shannon

To find out more about our authors and books visit www.hartpublishing.co.uk.
Here you will find extracts, author information, details of forthcoming events
and the option to sign up for our newsletters.

For Susie

FOREWORD

The French acquired a code of commercial law in 1807, the *Code de Commerce* being intended to supplement the *Code Civil* introduced three years before and building on the *Ordonnance de Commerce* of 1673. Work on the US Uniform Commercial Code began with the formation of the Uniform Law Commission in 1892, leading to a series of uniform laws for the key types of commercial transaction, and the Universal Commercial Code in 1951.

By contrast those purchasing a collection of statutes on commercial law in England and Wales will find legislation dealing with specific types of commercial transaction (the Sale of Goods Act 1979, the Bills of Exchange Act 1882 and so forth), statutes whose provisions vary (or used to, until the Consumer Rights Act 2015) depending on whether or not the contract they are being applied to is, or is not, a consumer contract and the absence until 2015 of avowedly consumer legislation.

This does not mean that, while England and Wales have a Commercial Court and commercial lawyers aplenty, it has no distinct body of commercial law. It simply means it is necessary to look a little harder for its organising, and animating, principles, and the elements in commercial transactions whose direct or analogous application provide the distinct shape of the argument and determination in commercial disputes.

In *Key Ideas in Commercial Law*, William Day has done just that. He identifies the key concepts assembled to create commercial transactions – payment, transfer of title, limitations on transferability and negotiability – and those which determine when, and through whose activities, a binding transaction comes into existence.

The book provides an insightful analysis of one of the key functions of terms in commercial transactions – the allocation of the risk in relation to contractual performance, and the risk that one party may lack the financial means to meet its obligations. This is particularly to be welcomed. Commenting on a very topical theory for the categorisation and judicial 'in-filling' of commercial bargains, I once suggested that 'even long-term contracts which are properly to be classified as "relational" are likely nonetheless to be "risk-allocational"'.

Students will find this work stimulating, engaging and enlightening. Practitioners in commercial law will find nuanced and insightful articulations of their stock-in-trade. William Day is to be congratulated on producing it, an achievement even more notable given his wide range of professional and academic commitments.

Sir David Foxton
Judge in Charge of the Commercial Court
12 February 2023

CONTENTS

NB this book explores commercial law thematically and the reader is encouraged to adopt that order to follow the development of the key ideas. However, some may prefer to dip in and out of the book by reference to more familiar doctrinal groupings. An alternative way to read this book is as follows:

1

Context and Concepts

1. CONTEXT

Law can be divided into contextual and conceptual subjects. Contract and trusts are examples of the latter: the subjects are organised around particular legal ideas. Commercial law is an example of the former. It does not focus on a particular legal concept but is a label for the collection of rules and principles that apply to dealings between parties acting in the course of business.

Commercial parties trade in three things: property, services and credit. In all but the most basic of businesses, a commercial enterprise must have more than one individual empowered to transact on its behalf. The rules at the heart of commercial law are those which govern when and how a person (or another acting on their behalf) can bargain for property, services and credit, and to acquire, dispose of and create interests in assets.

Commercial dealings typically comprise the exchange of money for some form of performance, and that involves taking two types of risk. One party takes performance risk ('Will my counterparty give me the goods, services or credit, as promised?') and the other takes credit risk ('Will my counterparty pay, as promised?'). However, a primary obligation to pay money is itself a species of performance risk and, since the law usually provides secondary monetary obligations (ie damages) where goods or services or credit are not delivered as promised (or delivered defectively), non-monetary performance risk often evolves into a question of credit risk after breach. A further credit risk question is '*Can* my counterparty pay?'. This raises a different set of considerations revolving around the spectre of insolvency. In this book, the phrase credit risk is principally used in this latter sense.

Commercial law is clearly distinguishable from some other contexts, such as dealings between a commercial party and a consumer. Interactions where neither side is acting in the course of business, such as family law and most of public and tort law, are also clearly different contexts. Nonetheless, when defined as the law applying to dealings between parties in the course of business, commercial law is still a very broad category. Further, commercial life in the modern economy is highly specialised, and each specialism has developed different versions of the same rules, and even some special rules of their own. Specialisms include construction and infrastructure, energy and natural resources, financial services, information technology, insurance, intellectual property and maritime law, just to give a few examples.

This book does not go into the detail of each of these specialist areas. Rather, it is concerned with key ideas which pervade the whole of commercial law. These are explored through five themes: trade, transacting, title, performance risk and credit risk. Each of these are addressed in turn in the chapters which follow.

2. CONCEPTS

Although a contextual subject, concepts are nonetheless very important in commercial law. Commercial law uses conceptual building blocks from the law of obligations and property law.

The law of obligations is about the rights and obligations that govern relationships between people. Property law can be described in two different ways: it can be said to be about the rights governing the relationship between a person and an asset, or as being about rights which one person has against everyone else in respect of an asset (Hohfeld 1917). Obligations and property are not autonomous of each other. Proprietary rights can lead to non-proprietary rights. So, for example, where a property right is infringed, the remedy often sounds in damages, which is a personal obligation to pay money to the person who holds the property right. The law of obligations can also create or modify rights to property. For instance, contracts can transfer or create rights to property.

Legal concepts can be both obligational *and* proprietary. It is a matter of perspective. For example, as between the parties to a contract, a debt is a personal claim and belongs to the law of obligations. But, as against third parties, debts can be treated as property (Reid 1997, 233). There is also a debate about whether equitable interests (such as under a trust or the type of security known as a 'charge') belong in the law of obligations or property law. These arise where an ownership right is modified to require that someone other than the legal owner benefit from the asset. The beneficiary or chargee is generally described as having a property right of their own in equity, although there is a long-standing theory that this 'interest' is purely a question of personal obligation between beneficiary/chargee and trustee/chargor (Maitland 1936). Again, this might be treated as a matter of perspective. As between those privy to the trust or charge, the obligations could be characterised in some way as personal. However, as against third parties, the beneficiary or chargee is treated as having a form of property right – albeit perhaps more accurately described as being a 'right against a right', namely the beneficiary or chargee's right (in equity) against the trustee's or chargor's right (at law) to the asset (McFarlane and Stevens 2010).

THE LAW OF OBLIGATIONS

Obligations can be mapped as arising by way of response to the following events (Birks 2005, 24):

Consent	Wrongs	Unjust Enrichment	Other

The most important type of consensual obligation arises from contracts. Contracts are 'the foundation on which commercial law rests' (Goode and McKendrick 2020, 31). And a large part of contract law is also commercial law: much of the formative case law involves disputes between two commercial parties.

Contracts are agreements requiring reciprocity of action by both parties. However, contracts are far from the only form of consensual transaction seen in commercial dealings. For example, promises lacking in reciprocity can be enforced if in the form of a deed. Deeds are still frequently used in financial transactions; security interests, for example, are often created by deed, not contract. Other forms of non-contractual consensual obligations in commercial law include assignments, bailments and express trusts.

Wrongs arise where there is a breach of duty or infringement of a right. Torts and equitable wrongs fall into this category. Equitable claims are typically brought to vindicate equitable interests in property, but not always. For example, a claim for breach of confidence does not turn on there being 'property' in information.

Torts have a less prominent role in commercial law than elsewhere. While tort law protects the right to possession of property by the tort of conversion, this does not extend to 'pure intangibles' which cannot be possessed (*OBG Ltd v Allan* [2008] 1 AC 1). Further, few claims in tort permit recovery of pure economic loss, which is the main interest which commercial parties seek to protect. A claim for such loss in negligence is possible after *Hedley Byrne & Co Ltd v Heller & Partners Ltd* [1964] AC 465, but the relevant duty of care arises only in limited circumstances. Otherwise, the defendant's behaviour needs to be particularly culpable before pure economic loss can be recovered: for example, by causing loss by making a statement knowing or being reckless as to its truth (the tort of deceit); by intentionally taking steps to induce a breach of contract, often known as the '*Lumley v Gye* tort' after the leading case ((1853) 2 E&B 216); or by combining with others to take steps with the intention of causing harm (the torts of conspiracy).

Unjust enrichment has an important role to play in commercial law in determining when transactions should be upheld and when they should be reversed. A claimant in unjust enrichment seeks restitution of what has been transferred: either the specific thing transferred or its monetary equivalent. A transaction may be flawed because it was induced by a misrepresentation, or an illegitimate threat, or an abuse of influence. In such cases, the law considers the claimant's actual intention to have been impaired and so will not hold them to the bargain. In other cases, the claimant is entitled to restitution because the transfer was subject to certain conditions, and those conditions have not materialised. In yet further cases, the claimant had no relevant intention to enter into the transaction at all (eg they had no capacity to enter into the transaction). Unjust enrichment is thus a collection of claims united by the idea that there are circumstances in which parties might be restored to the position they were in before dealing with each other. In that sense, it is a looser conceptual category more like tort than the 'purer, tighter and more unified set of rules' seen in contract (Burrows 2019, 530; cf Stevens 2023).

PROPERTY LAW

Something becomes an asset or property when access to it can be controlled by a particular person (Gray 1991, 294). This ability to control property is expressed in the language of property rights. Above all else, property rights confer two things: (i) the ability to exclude others from the property and (ii) the ability to confer that right of access on someone else.

Property law can be mapped in a similar way as obligations: consent, wrongs and unjust enrichment are all events that can trigger proprietary interests, either in law or equity. However, property law may also be mapped by reference to type of property, as follows:

Land Law	Personal Property Law		
	Choses in possession	Choses in action	
		Documentary Intangibles	Pure Intangibles

Land law evolved first and separately from personal property law. Up to the early modern period in England, land was the principal source of wealth and economic activity. But the economy gradually shifted away from agrarian activity, and that change accelerated in the eighteenth and nineteenth centuries with the industrial revolution. Napoleon famously called England a 'nation of shopkeepers', which he later explained when in exile in St Helena to be a compliment: 'I meant that you were a nation of merchants, and that all your great riches, and your grand resources arose from commerce' (O'Meara 1822, 52).

As a result of these economic developments, personal property – meaning property other than land – became much more important in commercial terms, and the courts increasingly had to grapple with property disputes that were not concerned with land. Within personal property, 'choses in possession' are goods or chattels, that is, items of property that can be controlled through physical possession. Manufacture and international trade in goods were what drove the UK's economic growth during the Napoleonic wars and the industrial revolution.

'Choses in action' are property that cannot be possessed, where title has to be enforced through taking legal action. This category can be subdivided into two. 'Pure intangibles', such as most contractual debts and intellectual property rights, have no proprietary relation with any physical item. 'Documentary intangibles', such as certain documented contractual debts (for instance bills of exchange and promissory notes), arise where the intangible is treated as being embodied in a document and so dealing with the document (like any other chattel) amounts to dealing with the relevant intangible. The law took this approach to reflect and facilitate developing commercial practices.

In the modern economy, intangible property (including intellectual property) is now much more important in commercial terms than chattels or land. However, even in a service-orientated economy like England, the buying and selling of tangible assets between commercial parties still remains a very large part of the economy.

3. THEMES AND CONTROVERSIES

A number of themes and controversies run through each of the chapters that follow. Five merit brief introduction at the outset, although the reader may wish to come back to these again at the end:

(1) *Sources of commercial law*. Commercial law is in a sense like any other private law subject: it is made up of statute law built upon case law. Some statutes have sought to counter common law developments (for example, the attempts of the Insolvency Act 1986 to limit the strength of the floating charge: see page 140 below) and others have sought to codify the common law to make it more readily understandable to market participants (for example, the Sale of Goods Act 1893). But a distinctive feature of commercial law is its responsiveness to commercial practice, such that commercial practice has a function as a source of commercial law in its own right. Sometimes this takes the form of Parliament reacting to concerns in the commercial community: see, for example, the introduction of the Factors Acts 1823–1889 discussed at pages 82–84 below, or the reversal of Holt CJ's decision to reject the negotiability of promissory notes discussed at pages 35 below. Often, the dialogue has been directly between the market and the courts. Special mercantile juries were one way that this occurred (see pages 58, 61 and 104 below) before civil juries were abolished. The modern equivalent is the Commercial Court, which was set up in 1895 following demands

from the City of London and the business community for a tribunal or court staffed by judges with knowledge and experience of commercial disputes who could determine such disputes expeditiously and with the benefit of their experience from practice.

(2) *Principle and pragmatism.* This responsiveness of the common law to commercial practice means that the conceptual purity that may be craved by an academic lawyer can on occasion be sacrificed on the altar of commerciality. Lord Goff once said that 'the objective of the judges ... [is] to help businessmen, not to hinder them: we are there to give effect to their transactions, not to frustrate them: we are there to oil the wheels of commerce, not to put a spanner in the works, or even grit in the oil' (Goff 1984, 391). So, for example, when it was suggested that letters of credit may not be valid contracts for lack of consideration, the Supreme Court expressed itself willing to ignore that fundamental formation rule (see page 15 below). But there are limits to how far this goes, especially in property law. The Supreme Court was not moved in *Re Spectrum Plus Ltd* [2005] 2 AC 680 by the plea that a security arrangement should remain characterised as a fixed charge because of the difficulties for lenders that would be caused if it were recharacterized as a floating charge after some 20 years of practice (see further pages 141–42 below). And often there is not a clear single 'commercial answer' that can be supplied; instead, what the court (or Parliament) is instead faced with are competing claims by commercial parties as to where performance and credit risk ought to be allocated as between them. This leads onto the next theme.

(3) *Freedom of contract and default rules.* In most commercial disputes, the argument will not be about the law itself but rather about the parties' particular bargain. Most commercial disputes are focused on arguments about what the contractual terms are and mean, and what effect they have on the allocation of risk. But the parties' contract is not made in a vacuum. Rather, the parties have contracted against background of a series of default rules making up the body of commercial law. This goes further than simply the territory of terms implied by law in contracts, discussed in chapter five, although that is an important part of it. The effect of title passing in sale of goods contracts (see pages 17–21 below), certain rules about the authority of agents (see page 60 below) and even the *pari passu* principle in insolvency (see pages 129–33 below) can all also be regarded as forms of default rule. However, there is again a limit to this: some rules in commercial law are – or ought to be – mandatory

not permissive. For example, at common law, it is fundamental that property interests cannot be created or transferred without satisfying the three Certainties, and the statutory exception that has been created to this fundamental rule is far from satisfactory (see pages 22 and 30–32 below). Likewise, it might be thought that English law currently goes too far in allowing parties to strike their own course when mitigating against credit risk, which necessarily comes at a cost to the wider pool of creditors in an insolvency (see page 133 below).

(4) *Good faith and fair dealing.* Unlike many civil law jurisdictions, and the US Uniform Commercial Code, English law has no overarching doctrine of good faith but has 'characteristically, committed itself to no such overriding principle but has developed piecemeal solutions in response to demonstrated problems of unfairness': *Interfoto Picture Library Ltd v Stiletto Visual Programmes Ltd* [1989] QB 433, 439 (per Bingham LJ). This is sensible not least because it is never clear in any given context what is meant by 'good faith', and whether it is limited to honesty (for example, s 61(3) of the Sale of Goods Act 1979) or is to be taken to mean something more. Commercial law, as defined in this book, focuses on dealings between parties in the course of their *respective* businesses. In that context, doctrines that might be associated with dealing in good faith have an important but somewhat limited role. These arise in the context of rules on when title may pass in property dealings (see pages 77–81 and 88–89 below) and – through doctrines such as misrepresentation and duress – protecting freedom of contract by ensuring that parties' 'consent to the terms of the contract has been obtained fairly': *First Tower Trustees Ltd v CDS (Superstores International) Ltd* [2019] 1 WLR 637, at [104] (per Leggatt LJ). Good faith has a much greater role where the dispute between parties is *internal* to a single business. For example, those authorised to work on behalf of that business will owe fiduciary duties as agents (see pages 53–54 below). And the common law may now, as a default rule, imply obligations of good faith into joint venture agreements and similar arrangements where commercial parties are not dealing at arms-length but rather pursuing a common enterprise: see, for example, *Al Nehayan v Kent* [2018] EWHC 333 (Comm), at [167]–[176] (per Leggatt LJ). As Mr Justice Foxton alludes to in his foreword to this book, arguments over when a contract has become 'relational' are in reality about risk allocation in the same way as any other commercial dispute.

(5) *Certainty and objectivity*. One of the criticisms made of any good faith 'mission creep' in English commercial law is that it will introduce unpredictability into an area which prizes certainty. There is therefore a certain irony that Lord Mansfield, the founding father of English commercial law, who tried to introduce good faith into the common law – but failed beyond insurance contracts: *Carter v Boehm* (1766) 3 Burr 1905 – also emphasised that in 'all mercantile transactions the great object should be certainty: and therefore, it is of more consequence that a rule should be certain, than whether the rule is established one way or the other': *Vallejo v Wheeler* (1774) 1 Cowp 143, 153. Certainty remains a cornerstone principle and is seen as 'a traditional strength and major selling point of English commercial law': *Golden Strait Corp v Nippon Yusen Kubishika Kaisha (The Golden Victory)* [2007] 2 AC 353 at [1] (per Lord Bingham). And it is one reason often given for the overriding principle that parties' bargains are construed 'objectively' as they would be understood by a reasonable person, with the parties' actual or 'subjective' intended meaning for the words expressing their agreement being irrelevant and inadmissible. But the objective principle can *also* be explained on an agreement-centred theory of commercial law. Agreements are objective because communication is. Since commercial parties must express their intentions in order to deal with each other, they necessarily must use a shared meaning and, as a matter of practical compromise, the best that can be hoped for when we communicate is that the recipient discovers the apparently intended meaning of the words used (Hoffmann 1997, 661).

2

Trade

This chapter is about what commercial parties do with each other: trade. Trade involves the exchange of money for property, services and credit. Property transactions are in legal terms perhaps the most interesting because they sit on the fault line between contract law and property law, and so they reveal something about the inter-relation of the different conceptual building blocks of commercial law. However, an account of the law of trade would be incomplete without also considering trade in services and credit, which dominate the modern economy. First, however, we should address the question of payment, which is one side of every commercial transaction.

1. PAYMENT

Payment is the act tendered by the buyer of goods, services or credit to the seller, and accepted by the seller, in discharge of an obligation expressed in money terms. Usually that act is the provision of money itself, although it can be achieved in other ways, such as through the set-off of countervailing money obligations.

INTRODUCTION TO THE FUNCTIONS AND THEORIES OF MONEY

Money is best defined by reference to its functions. Aristotle famously identified three principal functions of money, arising from its fungibility:

(1) *A Medium of Exchange*, facilitating trade without resort to barter. Barter was obviously a highly inconvenient way to conduct trade. One party could only buy something from a counterparty if they had some

particular property which they were willing to exchange and that the counterparty wanted.

(2) *A Unit of Account*, being a denominator of economic value for goods and services. English law recognised this function of money early on. The Privy Council said in *Gilbert v Brett* (1605) Davis 18, 19, citing German scholarship that in turn drew on Aristotle's *Nicomachean Ethics*, 'by the medium of money there can be an agreed and proper price for all things in the world'.

(3) *A Store of Value*, enabling value to be spent when required and in the meantime amassed without losing value (albeit at money's nominal rate, and so vulnerable to inflation). That is to be contrasted with, for example, the value of precious metals from which coins are made, which rises and falls depending on supply and demand.

The role of the state in monetary systems – in England, through the Royal Mint for coinage and the Bank of England for banknotes – has led some to define money by reference only to those tokens fulfilling the three functions above that are *also* issued by the authority of the state (for example, Mann 1992, 8). In practice, however, the law has preferred a 'societal theory' to the identification of money, conferring that status on any medium which in practice is being used to fulfil these functions. It might be thought that the recent rise of cryptocurrencies also support the societal theory of money, but this depends on the purpose of investing in them; many commercial parties have bought into cryptocurrencies not with the intention of meeting payment obligations but rather as an investment, speculating on their future exchange rates with more conventional currencies.

COINS, BANK NOTES AND BANK MONEY

Banknotes provide an example of the societal theory in practice. These are a form of payment instrument, that is, a documented right to payment. We are now accustomed to banknotes in England and Wales only being issued by the Bank of England, and to banknotes in Scotland and Northern Ireland only being issued by a limited number of authorised banks. Historically, however, a banknote was a promissory note (that is, a contract) that could be made by *any* bank: a promise by that bank to pay the bearer a certain sum in coinage, originally issued to a customer of that bank, and then used by that customer as a form of payment with third parties.

The common law started treating banknotes as the monetary equivalent of coinage long before Parliament legislated to bring banknotes under state control. Both coins and banknotes benefited from a 'currency' rule: if the coin or note was exchanged in trade where the recipient was acting in good faith and without notice that the money might be stolen (or that there could be some other title defect) then the recipient obtained a fresh legal title, better than any other coming before. See *Miller v Race* (1758) 1 Burr 452, discussed further at pages 35–36 below.

Another example of the societal approach to money in law is that money may cease to be money if it is not being treated as such. In *Moss v Hancock* [1899] 2 QB 111, a thief stole a £5 gold coin minted to commemorate Queen Victoria's Golden Jubilee and sold it on to a dealer in collectible items who bought it for five sovereigns. The victim sued for its return. The dealer had acted in good faith and without notice, and so sought to rely on the currency rule. This was rejected by the Court. Both the thief and the dealer had treated the coin, when dealing with it, as a collectible item in itself rather than as fungible money that could be paid in discharge of a £5 debt. The coin had therefore not passed into currency.

A further challenge to the state theory of money is that, in the modern economy, the vast majority of commercial transactions do not use coins or notes *at all*. Instead, payment is by bank transfer. Bank money is the contractual debt owed by the bank to its customer, represented by the value of the balance in the customer's account: *Foley v Hill* (1848) 2 HL Cas 28. A bank transfer from A to B involves an adjustment downwards of the balance in A's bank account and an adjustment upwards of B's bank account (and corresponding adjustments as between A and B's banks, and any intermediary institutions in the banking system): *R v Preddy* [1996] AC 815. A bank transfer therefore involves a pure transfer of value, without the physical transfer of any token or property rights.

BILLS OF EXCHANGE AND LETTERS OF CREDIT

In addition to bank notes, commercial parties developed other payment instruments for international trade. Bills of exchange were first developed

by Italian merchants carrying on trade across Medieval Christendom in
the thirteenth century. They are still a feature of modern commercial law.
A bill is an unconditional order requiring payment of a certain sum to
the bearer of the bill. The seller would be made the bearer of the bill, and
so the beneficiary of the order given by, or on behalf of, the buyer to the
buyer's bank (or another bank which had a relationship with the buyer's
bank) to make payment.

Letters of credit are a further payment mechanism regularly used in
international trade to mitigate against credit risk. The purpose of a letter of credit is to enhance the prospect of payment. In addition to the
buyer's payment obligation, the beneficiary (seller) obtains from a bank
(or banks) a freestanding and irrevocable right to prompt payment upon
receipt of the stipulated trade documents, regardless of any dispute which
the applicant (buyer) may raise under the underlying sale contract. The
bank thus acts a 'reliable and solvent paymaster' (*Soproma SpA v Marine
and Animal By-Product Corporation* [1966] 1 Lloyd's Rep 367, 385), giving the seller confidence to ship and then release the goods.

The documents which the seller must present to the bank to obtain
payment must strictly comply with what has been stipulated. There is
'no room for documents which are almost the same, or which will do
just as well': *Equitable Trust Co of New York v Dawson Partners Ltd* (1927)
27 Ll L Rep 29, 52 (per Viscount Sumners). So, for example, although
'Coromandel groundnuts' and 'machine-shelled ground kernels' are the
same thing, if the letter of credit requires a bill of lading for the former
and the bill of lading in fact states the latter, the bank is entitled to refuse
payment: *JH Rayner & Co Ltd v Hambro's Bank Ltd* [1943] KB 37. This
rule of strict compliance is to allow the bank to make quick decisions,
and not get into the detail of the underlying transaction, or be exposed
to the risk of making payment for the wrong goods. In practice, however,
where there is a non-conforming presentation of documents, the terms
of the credit will usually permit a period of time in which the bank can
take instructions from the buyer as to whether to waive the discrepancy.
If the documents comply, or if a waiver is given by the buyer, the bank
will then make payment and release the documents to the buyer so that
they can take delivery at the port of destination.

Opening a credit involves a matrix of contracts. The buyer has to secure
a credit facility with the bank issuing the credit. The seller likewise has a
relationship with its own bank, which either assumes no payment obligations of its own (an 'advising bank') or also promises to pay on receipt of

the stipulated trade documents (a 'confirming bank'). Although the seller is the beneficiary under the credit, and can enforce its right to payment on default by the issuing bank, it will be noted that the seller provides no consideration to the issuing bank. Despite this, the Supreme Court has said it would be 'loath to hold, particularly in a commercial context, that a promise which both parties intended should be relied on was unenforceable for want of consideration': *Taurus Petroleum Ltd v State Oil Marketing Co of the Ministry of Oil, Iraq* [2018] AC 690, at [25] (per Lord Clarke). This is a good example of legal dogma bending to facilitate commercial practice.

Central to a letter of credit's effectiveness as a method of payment is the 'autonomy principle', by which the credit is treated as being autonomous from the other contracts in the matrix. This means payment cannot be refused because of some underlying dispute between buyer and seller about the goods. As May LJ explained in *Sirius International Insurance Co (Publ) v FAI General Insurance Ltd* [2003] 1 WLR 2214, at [26]:

> Because the letter of credit is, subject to its terms, the equivalent of cash, the bank is not concerned with any disputed question, not within the terms of the letter of credit itself, which may arise under the underlying sale contract between the seller and the buyer ... This is the autonomous nature of letters of credit. By means of it, banks are protected and the cash nature of letters of credit is maintained.

However, a limited number of exceptions have been developed to the autonomy principle:

(1) *Fraud*. If the seller presents fraudulent documents to the bank (that is, documents containing deliberate and material misstatements to the knowledge of the seller), the bank is entitled to refuse payment: *United City Merchants (Investments) Ltd v Royal Bank of Canada* [1983] 1 AC 168 (HL). On one view, this is not really an exception to the autonomy principle at all, because the fraudulent statement is being made to the bank pursuant to the letter of credit. It is not yet clear whether fraud only in the underlying sales transaction would *also* permit the bank to refuse payment. This would be an unattractive development, drawing the bank into the relationship between buyer and seller (though see Enonchong 2011, 101–04; Goode and McKendrick 2020, 1119–20).

(2) *Nullity*. What if the seller unknowingly presents fraudulent documents to the bank? It has been suggested that the bank should still be entitled to refuse payment if the documents are a nullity (Goode and

McKendrick 2020, 1123–25). A nullity exception was recognised in *Beam Technology (Mfg) Pte Ltd v Standard Chartered Bank* [2003] 1 SLR 597. It has been suggested that this is a 'limited' exception which only applies where (i) a material document, (ii) was forged, (iii) the bank knew of the forgery and (iv) the bank had not already accepted the document (Enonchong 2011, 150–51). But that definition is in tension with *Beam Technology* itself, where Chao JA said at [36] that the question of nullity 'can only be answered on the facts of each case', with generalisation impossible. That gives banks and buyers little guidance or certainty as to when there may be a departure from the autonomy principle. Fortunately, the Court of Appeal in England has rejected a nullity exception: *Montrod Ltd v Grundkötter Fleischvertriebs GmbH* [2002] 1 WLR 1965.

(3) *Unconscionability.* Singapore has also moved towards recognising a broader unconscionability exception beyond fraud and nullity, where the demand for payment might be said to be unconscionable or lacking in good faith: see, for example, *GHL Pte Ltd v Unitrack Building Construction Pte Ltd* [1999] 4 SLR 604. There is a single first instance decision in England which also recognises this exception: *TTI Team Telecom International Ltd v Hutchison 3G UK Ltd* [2003] 1 All ER (Comm) 914. However, these have been in cases of 'performance bonds', where letters of credit mechanics have been adapted into a form of guarantee (see page 144 below) rather than in the context of financing trade. It remains to be seen whether the exception extends to letters of credit: if so, it could substantially undermine their 'cash like' status.

(4) *Illegality.* The autonomy principle should mean that, even if the underlying sales transaction is illegal, the seller should be able to call for payment under the credit. That has obvious public policy implications. In *Mahonia Ltd v JP Morgan Chase Bank* [2004] EWHC 1927 (Comm), a letter of credit was issued in support of a derivatives transaction. It was alleged that the underlying derivatives transaction was illegal for being in breach of US securities legislation. While that allegation was dismissed at trial, it was established that, if it had been true, that would have furnished a good reason not to pay on the credit. That must be right: the commercial utility of the autonomy principle cannot override the legality of the overall transaction.

(5) *Contrary Terms.* Like all contracts, the parties can create their own exceptions to the autonomy principle or dispense with it altogether. This is what was at issue in *Sirius International* itself, where the Court of

Appeal injuncted the seller drawing payment due to terms contained a side agreement which carved out an exception to the autonomy principle (the injunction was eventually overturned by the House of Lords, but on a different point).

2. TRADE IN GOODS

WHY TRANSFER OF TITLE MATTERS

The transfer of ownership to goods is the essence of trade in goods. That is what the buyer is paying for. This is illustrated by *Rowland v Divall* [1923] 2 KB 500 (CA). The claimant dealt in cars, bought one from the defendant, and then sold it on to one of his customers two months later. It was later discovered that the car had been stolen, and the defendant had no title to transfer to the claimant. The claimant sued the defendant for restitution of the purchase price on the basis that the consideration (that is, the condition on which the money had been paid) had totally failed. The defendant argued that there had been no *total* failure of consideration because the claimant had nonetheless had the benefit of possessing the car for a couple of months. The Court of Appeal had no time for that argument. As Atkin LJ put it (at 506–07), the buyer 'has not got any part of that for which he paid the purchase money. He paid the money in order that he might get the property, and he has not got it … The whole object of a sale is to transfer property from one person to another'.

The question of whether when there has been a transfer of a title is important for at least five further reasons:

(1) *Frustration.* Transfer of title matters if there are arguments about whether the contract might be discharged for frustration arising from an event that has occurred after the contract has been agreed. Take a contract for specific goods. If those specific goods are destroyed by accident, the contract will be discharged for frustration if title remains with the seller, because only transfer of title to the destroyed asset would have constituted performance under the contract. Conversely, if the title had already been transferred to the buyer at the time of destruction, performance would have already been rendered and there would be nothing left to frustrate: s 7 of the Sale of Goods Act 1979. (In this chapter, all

statutory references are to the 1979 Act, unless otherwise stated or obvious from the context.)

While the fashionable theory of frustration is it that constitutes a rule of law based on fairness to the parties, the better view is that it is a product of the agreed allocation of contractual risk between the parties (Day 2023). According to this older 'construction theory' of frustration, the law looks at the express and implied terms of the contract to determine whether the parties had envisaged continued contractual performance in the events which have transpired. Consistent with this, s 7 itself recognises that the contract will not be frustrated if specific goods were destroyed before title was transferred where risk passed by agreement to buyer before title. (Implied allocations of risk also explain cases usually attributed to a doctrine of 'common mistake', codified by s 6: see Morgan 2018.)

Title therefore supplies a rule as to when the contract should be discharged by the supervening event, but only a default rule that can be changed by other contractual terms. Rooting frustration in the terms of the contract in this way helps make sense of otherwise difficult cases, such as *Howell v Coupland* (1876) 1 QBD 258, where the seller agreed to sell 200 tons of potatoes grown on his 68 acre Lincolnshire farm. A disease ravaged the farm, and the seller was only able to produce less than 80 tons. The Court of Appeal held that the seller was not in breach for failing to provide the remaining 120 tons because (per Lord Coleridge CJ, at 261):

> there should be a condition implied that before the time for the performance of the contract the potatoes should be, or should have been, in existence, and should still be existing when the time came for the performance ... It was not an absolute contract of delivery under all circumstances, but a contract to deliver so many potatoes, of a particular kind, grown on a specific place, if deliverable from that place.

Sir Mackenzie Chalmers, the draftsman of the original Sale of Goods Act 1893 (from which the 1979 Act largely derives), considered this case to be within the scope of what became s 7 (Chalmers 1890, 11). However, this is problematic because s 7 only applies to specific goods, and potatoes to be grown on a farm are not obviously specific goods. *Howell v Coupland* is better viewed as a case which simply turned on the terms of the contract, as is the case for frustration generally.

The construction theory of frustration also assists with cases which are subject to the wider common law test for frustration. In *Blackburn Bobbin*

Co Ltd v Allen & Sons [1918] 2 KB 467 a contract to deliver Finnish birch timber to the buyer in Hull was not frustrated by the outbreak of the First World War, despite the fact that the conflict made it impossible for the seller to obtain timber from Finland. Pickford LJ pointed out (at 469) that 'it was no concern of the buyers as to how the sellers intended to get the timber there'. Conversely, had the contract stipulated how or when the timber was to be transported from Finland to Hull, the outcome would have been different. The outcome therefore simply reflected the terms of the contract.

(2) *Bearing the cost of damage or loss.* Whoever is title-holder to property generally takes the 'risk' (meaning, in this context, bears the cost) if the property is damaged or lost: s 20(1). So, for example, in *Underwood Ltd v Burgh Castle Brick and Cement Syndicate* [1922] 1 KB 343 a 30 ton condensing machine was badly damaged by its seller when loading it onto the train for delivery but contended that the buyer should bear the cost. In *Pignataro v Gilroy* [1919] 1 KB 459 bags of rice were stolen after the seller had set them aside for the buyer, but before the buyer was able to collect them. As we will see in this chapter (see pages 25–26 and 28 below), the law resolved both cases by asking whether title had passed to the buyer at the time of the accident. As a starting point this makes sense. It is part of what it means to have a property right: the title-holder is the party with the economic interest in the asset at law.

Again, however, this is only a default rule. The parties can expressly or impliedly agree otherwise. And the law seems relatively willing to imply such an agreement. This is the best justification for the now-codified rule that the buyer who demands delivery at a different place to the sale takes the risk of deterioration in the goods necessarily incidental to that transit: s 33(1).

There are other (uncodified) examples of implied agreements in the case law that displace the default rule. For example, in *Head v Tattersall* (1870) LR Ex 7, the claimant bought a horse on a Monday with the right to return it by the Wednesday. Through no fault of the defendant, the horse met with an accident the same day and was injured. The claimant was nonetheless still entitled to return the horse: the seller had impliedly retained the risk even whilst (temporarily) passing title.

Stern Ltd v Vickers Ltd [1923] 1 KB 78 is an example of the converse arrangement: title remained with the seller but the parties impliedly agreed that risk passed to the buyer. The seller sold 120,000 gallons of white spirit from bulk in a specific tank and provided the buyer with a delivery warrant. Under the statutory rules then in operation, discussed at pages 27–29 below, title could not pass whilst the goods were still an unidentified part of a wider bulk. The buyer did not want to take delivery, so agreed to paid for it to stay in the tank at the warehouse. After some time, it was discovered that it had been contaminated and had partly evaporated. Scrutton LJ held that risk had passed since the sellers had done everything they could do, and had lost control of the property, even though title had not passed.

Control seems to be the key to the finding of an implied agreement in *Stern v Vickers*. *Healy v Howlett & Sons* [1917] 1 KB 337 involved very similar facts – albeit with fish rather than white spirit – but no delivery warrant had been issued, so control had not been conferred on the buyer. It was held that risk had remained with the seller.

The other exceptions to the presumption that risk follows title apply where one or other party is at fault, such as where the loss arises from the wrongdoing (such as breach of contract or negligence) of the buyer or seller. But wrongdoing is only one type of fault in this context. Where title has not passed because of delayed delivery, which is the fault of one of the parties, then some risk falls on that party (s 20(2)). When goods are in transit, the seller is at risk if it has entered into an unreasonable contract with the carrier (s 32(2)) or has failed to notify the buyer before a sea transit to enable the buyer to take out insurance (s 32(3)).

(3) *Control of the asset and claims against third parties.* The transfer of title confers with it a right to control access to it. In particular, title confers an entitlement to possession of the goods, and so the transferee can bring a claim in the tort of conversion or trespass to goods, even if the asset has not yet been delivered. Title is also relevant to claims in negligence. In *The Aliakmon* [1986] AC 785, goods were badly stowed on board the vessel and damaged at sea. The buyer sued and its claim was dismissed: under the terms of the sales contract, risk had passed but title had remained with the sellers. That was not good enough. As Lord Brandon explained (at 809):

> in order to enable a person to claim in negligence for loss caused to him by reasons of loss of or damage to property, he must have had either the legal ownership of or a possessory title to the property concerned at the time when the loss or damage occurred, and it is not enough for him to have had only contractual rights in relation to such property which have been adversely affected by the loss of or damage to it.

(4) *Credit risk.* If title has not passed and the buyer enters into an insolvency process, the seller runs the risk of being an unsecured creditor; the value in the asset can be realised by the insolvency officeholder for the benefit of all creditors. In contrast, if title has not passed, and the buyer enters into an insolvency process, the seller can hold onto the property because it does not form part of the buyer's insolvent estate and therefore not something which the officeholder can realise.

The buyer can also be concerned about credit risk. *Re Wait* [1927] 1 Ch 606 is a salutary example. Wait bought 1,000 tons of wheat and sold on 500 tons to various sub-purchasers before it arrived. The sub-purchasers paid Wait, but he became bankrupt before the wheat was delivered. The 500 tons could not be ascertained from the wider 1,000 tons so title did not pass under the relevant rules (discussed at pages 27–29 below) so the sub-purchasers were left as unsecured creditors in Wait's bankruptcy rather than being able to ringfence 500 tons of the wheat from the bankruptcy estate as belonging to them.

Credit risk is considered further in chapter six. But, as we will see in this chapter, concerns about the risk of insolvency has also driven changes to the very rules as to when title will be transferred.

(5) *Buyer's power and right to sell the asset on to another.* If the buyer has been transferred title, he will normally have the right and power to transfer that title onto another. This is discussed in chapter four. If the buyer has not yet received title, he will not have the power to transfer title (unless there is an exception to *nemo dat*) and, similarly, he is less likely to have the right to do so.

US realists deplore the common law's heavy reliance on title (see, for example, Llewellyn 1938). That view has attracted some support in this jurisdiction. For example, the law on consumer sales has now decoupled risk from title and instead attached it to the transfer of possession: see Consumer Rights Act 2015, s 29.

Scholars like Llewellyn have a point that some parts of sales law historically made links to title which made no sense. One obvious nonsense in English law was the apparent requirement under s 49 that, whatever the terms of the contract, an action for the price could only be sustained where title had been transferred (subject to an exception where the price was otherwise payable on a day certain). It is not clear that is right: the language of s 49 appears to be permissive rather than mandatory. The Supreme Court has, rightly, suggested that there can be exceptions – albeit narrow ones – to s 49 (*PST Energy 7 Shipping LLC v OW Bunker Malta* [2016] AC 1034, [58] (per Lord Mance)), although only in *obiter dicta*, so it may be argued that the *ratio* to the contrary in an earlier Court of Appeal decision remains better authority (*FG Wilson (Engineering Ltd v John Holt & Co (Liverpool) Ltd* [2014] 1 WLR 2365, [52] (per Longmore LJ)). More broadly, however, this criticism as to the impact of title can be taken too far. For each of five points discussed above, the better view is that these consequences can be justified by reference to what it means to have a property right in goods, and how that then plays out in the context of tort, contract and insolvency law.

PRINCIPLES OF TITLE TRANSFER

There is a trilogy of 'Certainties' which must be satisfied before any property interest can be transferred. First, *certainty of intention*. That is, did the title-holder intend to transfer title? Second, *certainty of subject matter*. That is, what property did the title-holder intend to transfer title? Third, *certainty of object*. That is, to whom did the title-holder intend to transfer property? In this book, these will be called 'Intention Certainty', 'Subject Matter Certainty' and 'Object Certainty'. They also apply to the creation of property interests, such as security rights discussed in chapter six.

(1) *Abstract model.* The common law's original approach – borrowed perhaps from Roman law (or at least consistent with it) – was that property law rather than the contract law would dictate when title would pass from one party to another. Put another way, the property questions were separate or (to borrow from civilian thinking) 'abstract' from the contract, so it did not matter if the contract was void or voidable. In particular, for choses in possession, title would pass upon delivery as a matter of property law.

Delivery in property law has two components: (i) the transfer of possession of the goods by the title-holder to another and (ii) an intention by the title-holder to transfer that title to the other alongside transferring possession. So delivery is in turn contingent on the concept of *possession*. The common law has adopted a Roman law approach to possession. It means effective control of the goods for one's own benefit and to the exclusion of others and an intention so to control the goods (Pollock and

Wright 1888, 13–14). At its most basic, the transfer of possession involves person A handing over goods to person B. This is a bilateral act, involving a 'giving up' by person A and an 'acceptance' by person B. But the law has long recognised equivalent forms of transfer. Handing over a symbol of control such as a key or a document of title (such as a bill of lading) will suffice to constitute delivery, so long as accompanied by the necessary intention to transfer title. If the goods are held by person C, that person can 'attorn', that is, communicate that they are now holding the goods for B rather than A. This should be understood as C ceasing to act as agent or bailee for A and becoming the agent or bailee for B. These alternatives are sometimes called 'constructive' delivery, in contrast to 'actual' transfer or delivery.

Under the abstract model, Subject Matter and Object Certainty are answered by the act of transfer itself, leaving Intention Certainty to be assessed separately. The question of whether there is relevant intention is assessed objectively. The title-holder must intend to transfer title, not just possession, and the recipient must intend to receive title, not just possession. A transfer itself is inherently ambiguous so the assessment as to intention is necessarily of the wider conduct of the parties and the communications passing between them. For example, possession to the goods might have been transferred as a gift, or for repair, or as a loan; only in the first of those examples would there be the necessary intention to trigger the transfer of title. There is debate about whether, within this abstract model for the passing of title, intention can ever be vitiated, such as by fundamental mistakes such as to identity, subject-matter or quantity (see, for example, Fox 1996; Swadling 2006). Space preludes further discussion here, although it is fair to say that there is limited authority on the point, given the dominance of the causal model, to which we now turn.

(2) *Causal model.* Scottish law has always been more open to Roman law influences and so remained faithful to the abstract model (at least, until Chalmers interfered with it through the Sale of Goods Act 1893). However, the English common law long ago recognised that the Certainties can be satisfied entirely by consensual obligation. This removed the link between delivery and transfer of title. This is often known as the causal model. Its earliest (medieval) manifestation was probably transfer by way of deed. Transfer by way of contract was possible, at the latest, by the Elizabethan era: *Cochrane v Moore* (1890) 25 QBD 57, 71 (per Fry LJ).

By the time Chalmers came to draft the Sale of Goods Act 1893, he described the rule that title could be transferred by the intentions of the parties as embodied in a contract as being 'as old as the year books' (Chalmers 1890, 27) and he saw no reason not to impose it on Scotland as well, despite only purporting to be on a codifying mission. Chalmers' enthusiasm for the causal model was probably because he was working at a time when the 'will theory' developed by another civilian jurist, Robert-Joseph Pothier, exerted a hegemonic influence over English lawyers – indeed, in the introduction to his original book on the sale of goods, Chalmers noted that Pothier's authority on contract law was 'as high as can be had next to the decision of a Court of Justice in this country' (Chalmers 1890, vi–vii).

Under the causal model, the question of when title is transferred can be answered by looking at the objective intentions of the promisor in the deed or the parties to the contract. It might be before, at the same time as, or after, delivery. The central relevance of the 'will' on a causal transfer is underlined by the fact that, if the causal obligation is rescinded (eg for misrepresentation, duress or undue influence), then the transfer of title itself will *also* be unwound to effect restitution to reverse an unjust enrichment.

All this is by way of setting out the intellectual context in which to approach and understand Chalmers' codification of the common law on sale of goods in the Sale of Goods Act 1893, now consolidated in substantially its original form in the Sale of Goods Act 1979.

Chalmers' codification involves drawing a distinction between trade in *specific* and *unascertained* goods, and these are taken in turn below.

TRADE IN SPECIFIC GOODS

Where goods are specific, all three Certainties are satisfied within the four corners of the contract rather than by reference to delivery. Specific goods are those 'identified and agreed' at the time of contracting: s 61(1). Since 1995, the statutory definition has been expanded to include goods identified as an undivided share (eg 'two thirds' of the three tonnes of coal, rather than two of the three tonnes of coal).

For specific goods, only title to the particular goods – and not any goods answering the contractual description – can be transferred to discharge the seller's obligations under the contract of sale. By definition, therefore, a contract for specific goods will have Subject Matter Certainty. And the fact of the counterparty to the contract answers the need for Object Certainty. The terms of the contract also provide the requisite Intention Certainty. Title will transfer when the parties agree it will transfer. That involves an exercise in examining the contract's express and implied terms: s 17. It is open to the parties to agree that title will not pass until certain conditions are fulfilled, such as payment of the price, and that, if those conditions are not fulfilled, the seller can re-sell the property to someone else: s 19. Nowadays most commercial sellers deal on such retention of title ('RoT') terms because it mitigates the risk of being an unsecured creditor in the buyer's insolvency. This is discussed further in chapter six.

Whether using RoT terms or not, in the modern commercial world, sellers will typically sell on standardised terms which will expressly state when title is intended to pass. In 'f.o.b.' contracts, title usually passes on shipment; conversely, in 'c.o.b.' contracts, typically title only passes on payment. And even where the express terms say nothing, the court will willingly imply a term that title does not pass until the later of delivery or payment: *RV Ward Ltd v Bignall* [1967] 1 QB 534, 545 (per Diplock LJ). However, there are (comparatively rare) circumstances in which the contract is genuinely silent on this point. Here, s 18 supplies four default rules fill any gap in the contract.

(1) *Rule 1* applies to unconditional contracts where the goods are in a deliverable state at the time of contracting. Under rule 1 title passes on the conclusion of the contract. Unconditional contracts are contracts where the passing of title has not been contingent on some other matter, such as payment. Goods are in a 'deliverable state' where there is nothing left to be done to them before other than tender delivery. It is a test about completion of contractual commitments by the seller rather than asking whether the goods are 'deliverable in the sense that it is properly packed or anything of that kind': *Underwood Ltd v Burgh Castle Brick and Cement Syndicate* [1922] 1 KB 123, 125 (per Rowlatt J).

Underwood involved a 30 ton condensing machine which had been bolted into concrete. Rowlatt J held that title to the condensing machine did not transfer on sale because the parties had agreed it had to be unbolted from the concrete before it could be tendered for delivery. On appeal ([1922] 1 KB 343, 345), Bankes LJ may have become distracted by the size of the machines, noting that deliverable state also 'depends on the actual state of the goods'. Following *Underwood*, some later judges have doubled-down on a physical test for deliverability: see, for example, the very heavy carpet in *Philip Head & Sons Ltd v Showfront Ltd* [1970] 1 Lloyd's Rep 140. But this is misconceived: in *Underwood* itself, Bankes LJ went on to contrast the 'actual state of the goods' with the 'state in which they are to be delivered by the terms of the contract', which suggests he was not really saying anything different from Rowlatt J at first instance.

(2) *Rule 2*, in contrast to rule 1, contains a negative proposition. Where there is some matter outstanding before the goods are in a deliverable state, title does 'not pass' until it has been done and notice has been given. A negative rule is not much help in circumstances where the parties will only look to rule 2 when asking for positive guidance as to when title will pass and finding no answer in the express or implied terms of the contract. For this reason, the courts have tended to gloss rule 2 and treat it as a positive rule. In *Underwood*, for example, if the condensing machines had been unbolted and loaded onto a train ready to be transported from London to Yarmouth, as agreed, title would then have passed to the buyer (and also if notice had been given – although that is not clear from the law report).

(3) *Rule 3*, again, is framed in negative terms but treated by the courts as a positive proposition. Where the goods are in a deliverable state, but the seller has to do something to ascertain the price (eg weigh, measure or test them), title does 'not pass' until the seller has done that thing and given notice. Of course, often goods may be weighed, measured, or tested for reasons other than determining the price, and, if so, rule 3 does not apply. In *Nanka-Bruce v Commonwealth Trust Ltd* [1926] AC 77, for example, cocoa was weighed on delivery to check the correct quantities had been delivered. In *Nanka-Bruce*, there was a further reason why rule 3 could not apply: the relevant acts were to be done by the buyer not the seller. This seems arbitrary but is the irresistible result of Chalmers rejecting Lord Blackburn's sensible view, albeit expressed extra-judicially, that this rule should be extended to all acts undertaken to ascertain the price, whoever is performing them: Chalmers 1890, 31.

(4) *Rule 4* applies to contracts for sale or return or sale on approval. Title passes on (i) an act of 'approval', 'acceptance' or 'adoption' (it is difficult to see how these three words do not mean the same thing) or

(ii) the expiry of a reasonable period of time for rejection. There are rule 4 cases where the terms provide for a sales contract from the outset (for example, *Head v Tattersall* (1870) LR Ex 7, discussed at page 19 above). But more often than not, rule 4 contracts are contracts providing for an initial period of bailment coupled with an option to buy. They only become sales contracts when that option is triggered expressly, by communication of approval or acceptance or impliedly by 'adopting' the sales transaction (typically by doing something which goes beyond the terms of the bailment and prevents the return of the goods) or retaining the goods beyond a specified time or a reasonable time. This is therefore an oddity because the 1979 Act does not in fact apply to the initial contract. Further, once the option is triggered and the sales contract generated, if there are no other terms, rule 1 would usually be applicable, not rule 4.

TRADE IN UNASCERTAINED GOODS

In contrast to specific goods, title to goods cannot pass by contract alone when the contract is for the sale of goods which are unascertained: s 16. This is because, by definition, there can be no Subject Matter Certainty while the goods remain unascertained: any goods conforming to the terms of the contract could be tendered by the seller, and until tendered or otherwise ascertained there is insufficient certainty for title to pass. The fact that the contract terms show Intention and Object Certainty is not enough; all three Certainties must be met before there is a transfer. As Bovill CJ explained in *Heilbutt v Hickson* (1871–72) LR 7 CP 438, 449 'something more would generally remain to be done, such as, for instance, selection or appropriation, approval, and delivery of some kind, before the property would be considered as intended to pass, and upon that taking place the property might pass if it was intended to do so'. That 'something more' – which is necessarily extra-contractual – supplies Subject Matter Certainty which is missing from the contract itself.

An example is *Re London Wine Co (Shippers) Ltd* [1986] PCC 121 where wine was sold by the case to customers but retained in bulk in warehouses. Oliver J held that there was no Subject Matter Certainty because it was not possible to say which wine cases were attributable to any particular sales contract. Another example of a case where goods are unascertained is *Re Wait* [1927] 1 Ch 606 (discussed at page 21 above), where the sale was of 500 tons of wheat in a wider 1,000 ton bulk.

As Lord Harnworth MR said (at 622), 'there was no such identification of the thing, "the very thing", for the goods were not appropriated nor their individuality ascertained'. The lack of Subject Matter Certainty also led to the rejection of the alternative contention in *Re Wait* for a beneficial interest under a trust: the requirements for certainty for the creation of property interests in equity are the same as for the transfer of property rights at common law.

Section 18, rule 5 provides certain default rules as to when goods shift from being unascertained to ascertained. Subject to the contrary intention of the parties (for example, any RoT provisions) rule 5 envisages the passing of title occurring at the same time as that shift.

(1) *Rule 5(1)* provides that title will pass when goods answering the contractual description and in a deliverable state are 'unconditionally appropriated' to the contract by one party with the 'assent' of the other. *Appropriation* means that the goods must have been selected or ascertained. *Unconditional* appropriation means that that process cannot be reversed. That involves testing (objectively) the intention of the seller at the time of appropriation: the question is whether the seller was provisionally setting aside those goods for the sale, or whether the seller had made a final decision to transfer title to those goods to fulfil the sale.

So, for example, in *Pignataro v Gilroy* [1919] 1 KB 459, the seller agreed to sell the buyer bags of rice. The seller filled the bags and notified the buyer to collect them. It took around a month for the buyer to do so, and in the intervening period they had been stolen. It was held that title had passed: the notification showed that the appropriation was not just an act of internal organisation but a final selection of the particular goods to be sold. The buyer had impliedly assented by not expressing any objection to the notified appropriation. (For this reason, *Pignataro* is also authority for the proposition that the test for assent is not particularly exacting.)

By way of contrast, in *Carlos Federspiel & Co SA v Charles Twigg & Co Ltd* [1957] 1 Lloyd's Rep 240, the seller of bicycles put stock sufficient to meet a buyer's order into crates labelled for the buyer, but then went into receivership before those crates were put into transit by the seller. Pearson J said that a 'mere setting apart or selection of the seller of the goods which he expects to use in performance of the contract is not enough. If that is all, he can change his mind' (at 255). The judge went on to say that 'usually but not necessarily, the appropriating act is the last act to be performed by the seller' (also at 255). Put another way, if the seller has to do something else (such as notification or delivery) *after* the selection has been made, the selection itself is likely to be seen as simply a preliminary, internal organisational step rather than the final decision of the seller to transfer title to the particular goods in question.

(2) *Rule 5(2)* provides that title will pass when the goods are delivered to the buyer or a carrier for transmission to the buyer. It is drafted in the form of a deeming provision: delivery 'is to be taken' as unconditional appropriation. It might be thought to differ in substance from rule 5(1) because there is no freestanding requirement for assent by the counterparty. However, since delivery is a bilateral act where possession has to be accepted by the buyer the idea of assent is also inherent within it. In *Kulkarni v Manor Credit (Davenham) Ltd* [2010] EWCA Civ 69 at [22] and [44], Rix LJ characterised this as a 'long stop prima facie rule' which reflects an implied intention that delivery of the selected goods was to transfer both possession and property. However, the delivery must be completed in such a way as to make the goods ascertainable. In *Healy v Howlett & Sons* [1917] 1 KB 337, discussed at page 20 above, 190 boxes of mackerel were dispatched by train by the seller, 20 of which were for the buyer. The journey was delayed, and the fish began to rot. As the fish remained unascertained goods, the delivery to the carrier could not pass title (s 16) and so risk remained with the seller (s 20(1)).

(3) *Rules 5(3)–(4)* were added in 1995. These envisage that the goods will become ascertained from a wider bulk when the rest of the bulk has been used up. This is a codification of two cases decided since the time of Chalmers. In *Wait & James v Midland Bank* (1926) 31 Com Cas 172, it was held that the buyer's share in a bulk of wheat stored in a Bristolian warehouse became ascertainable after the seller had fulfilled all of their other orders. A similar result was reached in the *Karlshamns Olje Fabriker v Eastport Navigation Corp* [1982] 1 All ER 208, where various sellers shipped copra to the buyer on the vessel, *The Elafi*. Mustill J held that there was no need to segregate the goods as between the different contracts: the existence of the same buyer across the contracts conferred sufficient certainty of subject matter.

The best way to think about rules 5(1)–(4) is that the Certainties are completed by a *blend* of the causal and abstract models. The contract supplies Intention and Object Certainty, but not Subject Matter Certainty. Subject Matter Certainty instead comes from the parties' post-contractual acts with the goods. In abstract terms, these post-contractual matters have the same function as the act of delivery.

THE 1995 REFORMS

Chalmers' codification, set out above, was revised by the Sale of Goods (Amendment) Act 1995. We have already noted two of the more minor changes in the last section. A much more substantial change was made by ss 20A–20B to the 1979 Act, added by the 1995 Act, which creates an exception to s 16 – and the general requirement that the three Certainties be satisfied before title to property can be transferred.

The exception created by the 1995 Act has three preconditions (s 20A(1)). *First*, the contract must identify a bulk. A bulk is a mass of interchangeable goods of the same kind contained in the same space: s 61(1). So, the contract must point to something like a cargo of wheat in a particular ship, or oil in a particular tank, or bottles of the same wine in a particular cellar. A reference to 'general stock', in contrast, would not be enough. *Second*, the contract must be for 'specified quantity', that is, expressed as a number rather than as a fraction or percentage (eg, two of the three tonnes of coal, rather than 'two thirds' of the three tonnes of coal). *Third*, the buyer must have pre-paid at least some of the price for the goods: this reflects the underlying justification for the exception, considered next. On satisfaction of those three conditions, the buyer becomes an owner in common of the bulk, with a share within the bulk proportionate to the goods for which the buyer has paid: s 20A(2)–(3). This creates a holding or interim position; the buyer will then obtain an undivided interest in ascertained goods when the seller makes a delivery out of the bulk, thereby satisfying rule 5(2) of s 18.

The principal motivation behind the 1995 reform was to limit buyers' credit risk. The Law Commission considered there was an unfairness to the outcome of cases like *Re Wait* and *Re London Wine Co (Shippers) Ltd*, where the buyer paid the seller upfront only to find that the seller had gone insolvent (Law Commission 1993). Because title had not passed, the buyer would find themselves as being in the position of an unsecured creditor, and would probably only recover pence in the pound from the seller's liquidation. The creation of common ownership, as an interim position pending the ascertainment of the goods, was designed to protect against this credit risk.

It is not clear that the reform has entirely achieved what it set out to do. To avoid the co-ownership interests jamming up the seller's business, s 20B provides for deemed consent by the co-owners to the seller's dealings with the bulk. The unqualified and wide ambit of this deeming provision means that, when a seller gets into financial difficulty, buyers will race to secure ascertainment for themselves, leaving those slower off the mark with nothing or at least a reduced proprietary entitlement (Bridge 2019a, 72). This is not markedly better to the pre-1995 position where there would have been a similar rush by buyers to obtain their goods before a pending insolvency.

It is also not obvious that the reform was justified on its own terms. The problem with the Law Commission's case for reform is that it did not credibly explain why this class of unsecured creditor was more deserving of protection from credit risk than other classes of unsecured creditor – still less why these buyers should be protected *at the expense* of other unsecured creditors. It must be remembered that, if the goods are taken out of the seller's insolvent estate, they cannot be realised for the benefit of all creditors. The Law Commission pointed out that the principal creditors actually to suffer would be secured creditors with floating charges. But that still does not answer the fundamental question as to why the law should have been changed to protect buyers of bulk goods in priority to other creditors. In particular, there is no explanation as to why a class of creditors who have chosen not to bargain in such a way to mitigate credit risk should be placed above a class of creditors who have taken those precautions. As Atkin LJ stated in *Re Wait* (at 640):

> If a seller of goods delivers them to the buyer before payment, trusting to receive payment in due course, and the buyer becomes bankrupt, the seller is restricted to a proof, and can assert no beneficial interest in the goods. There seems no particular reason why a different principle should prevail where a buyer hands the price to the seller before delivery of the goods trusting to receive delivery in due course. In both cases credit is given to the debtor, and the buyer and the seller respectively take the well-known risk of the insolvency of their customer.

It might be said that it is harder for a buyer to bargain to mitigate credit risk against a seller who can, in contrast, impose RoT terms. But the buyer can always seek to have the goods on credit or have money held on trust an escrow account pending delivery. And it should be recalled that we are concerned here with commercial parties, not consumers who lack sophistication or bargaining power who may be more deserving of protection.

Against this, the Law Commission claimed (1992, 15): 'the reform is concerned with the rules on passing of property in sale transactions, not with the creation of a preference in insolvency. Insolvency law has to accept the rules of property law as it finds them'. This is unconvincing.

The reform was driven by a perceived problem about buyers' exposure to insolvency risk: the Law Commission chose to deal with it by adjusting property law, but it could just as well have done it by reforming insolvency law. The Law Commission continued (at 16): 'All that the proposed reforms is doing is removing an anomaly in the rules on the passing of property on sale.' However, that is simply wrong. As we have seen, all of the previous codified rules on the passing of property are justifiable by reference to the three Certainties. In contrast, the 1995 reforms do not comply with the Certainties principles, because Subject Matter Certainty does not have to be satisfied for title now to pass in goods. Viewed from that perspective, the 1995 reforms *create* rather than remove an anomaly.

In any event, there are a number of debatable points as to the operation of this exception to s 16 in practice. For present purposes, it suffices to note two. *First*, the method by which extent of the proprietary interest meant to be measured is not entirely clear. Should the proportions of various buyers be fixed on a rolling basis as the bulk is sold, or should the assessment be on the final date? The references in s 20A(3)–(4) to proportions 'at any time' relating to the quantity of goods paid for and in the bulk 'at that time' suggests the latter, and that is obviously the more practicable solution (Gullifer 2021, [20–023]).

Second, s 20A(4) provides that, if the bulk shrinks, so too does the buyers' proportionate shares, and they bear the risk of a shortfall *pro rata*. There is an unresolved debate as to whether any proportionate share belonging to the seller should share in the shortfall equally or should bear the loss first. The latter appears to have been the Law Commission's intention (Law Commission 1993, 21), and it is consistent with the omission of the seller from the express terms of s 20A(4). However, there are some powerful arguments to the contrary (Bridge 2019a, 65–69). In particular, as we have seen, under s 20(1) the usual rule is that risk follows title. In a co-ownership structure that should mean that all co-owners (buyers and sellers alike) bear the cost of damage or loss equally.

3. TRADE IN DEBTS

Choses in action can be traded in the same way as choses in possession. For the present purposes, we will focus on the type of chose in action traded most often: the debt.

DEBTS AS TRADEABLE PROPERTY
AT COMMON LAW

A debt is a right held by one person against another for payment of a certain amount of money at a specified point in time. The right is typically, but not always, created by contract. As discussed in chapter one, while a debt is between creditor and debtor a personal obligation, as against third parties a debt can be treated as property. That is because third parties can be excluded from the right to payment and also because debts can be traded. The latter point is central to the commodification of debts. It is no exaggeration to say that the evolution of debts into property is largely bound up in the development of legal mechanisms to allow parties to trade in debts.

Commercial parties have long treated rights to payment as assets which could be bought and sold. Legal systems have gradually developed rules giving effect to that commercial practice. The solution in Roman law by the time of Gaius was to allow a creditor to appoint another as their agent to collect the debt and then keep it for themselves; by Justinian's time, that artifice was unnecessary and the ability to transfer of debts was recognised in those terms by the law. As we will see, English law has undergone a similar evolution.

The common law was historically hostile to allowing the transfer of debts. That was partly because, as a matter of principle, rights to payment were seen as a personal matter between debtor and creditor rather than property that the creditor could trade (Holdsworth 1920, 1002–03). It was also because, in practice, debtors had an interest in their identity of their creditors. A friendly creditor might allow for late or part payment of a debt. But a hostile creditor could put a debtor in financial difficulty into an insolvency or, worse, imprisonment, as William Dorrit could attest. Moreover, there was a suspicion about the motives of those who wanted to buy into litigation, giving rise to the doctrine of maintenance, which remained a crime until abolished in 1967, but now has limited force as a common law doctrine.

Commercial parties nonetheless found ways to give effect at common law to the transfer of debts. The solution in the twelfth and thirteenth centuries combined pragmatism and prejudice: the common law allowed assignments of debts between Jewish financiers, and even to Christians so long as they sued in the name of the Jewish assignor (Bailey 1931).

After the expulsion of Jewish people in England by Edward I, medieval merchants then adopted an agency mechanism similar to that developed in Roman times.

THE DEVELOPMENT OF ASSIGNMENT AND NEGOTIABILITY

Equity was much more receptive to treating rights to payment as property. This was entirely unsurprising. Equity's greatest innovation is the trust. By the trust, one person (the trustee) could hold property for the benefit of another (the beneficiary). As discussed in chapter one, the nature of the beneficiary's right is controversial, but a good way of thinking about this is that the beneficiary holds a right against the trustee's right to the property. These structures were originally developed in medieval times for aristocratic landholdings, which were the great commercial enterprises of their day. But, by at least the late Tudor or early Stuart period, trusts were also regularly being used to hold other sorts of property *including debts* (Jones 2019, 325).

The recognition of debt as property in the context of trusts meant that the Chancery Court was also receptive to the idea of treating debts as property generally capable of assignment, subject to fulfilling the Certainties. That development had certainly happened by the start of the eighteenth century, and probably before: *Crouch v Martin & Harris* (1707) 2 Vern 595. Before the administrative fusion of the two branches of the law in the nineteenth century by the Judicature Acts of 1873 and 1875, the procedure for bringing a claim on an assigned debt was rather cumbersome. The assignee would bring an action against the assignor in the Chancery Court to obtain standing then to bring an action in the common law courts in the assignor's name.

Equity's innovations were followed in turn by innovation from the common law judges. By the late seventeenth century, merchants and other commercial parties had started treating certain debts as being embodied by their documented terms and therefore tradable by the physical transfer of the document itself. An early example of these 'negotiable instruments' was the bill of exchange, discussed earlier (see pages 13–14 above), which was central to financing international trade for centuries. If a merchant did not want to wait until the payment date, they would sell the bill of exchange at a discount to someone else who was willing to wait until the payment date to realise a return more quickly. This practice then extended to promissory notes and other documented debts. The common law had no problem in absorbing that mercantile practice: the physical transfers of these payment instruments obviously satisfied the Certainties.

However, the market received a shock when Holt CJ objected to conflation of promissory notes with bills of exchange, remarking that this was 'a new form of specialty, unknown to the common law, and invented in Lombard Street': *Clerke v Martin* (1702) 2 Ld Raym 758. Parliament quickly intervened by statute in 1704 to reverse his decision, and the founding father of modern commercial law, Lord Mansfield, extended the principle of negotiability yet further in the second half of the eighteenth century. In contrast to Holt CJ, Lord Mansfield emphasised that the common law should not 'clog' the negotiability of these debts given that they had been singled out in mercantile custom 'from all other contracts, by making them assignable … for the convenience of commerce': *Heylyn v Adamson* (1758) 2 Burr 669.

THE DECLINE IN THE COMMERCIAL IMPORTANCE OF NEGOTIABILITY

Although both satisfy the three Certainties, the approach taken to dealing with debts at common law ('negotiability') is radically different to the approach taken in equity ('assignment').

The common law approach is narrower. It does *not* apply to all debts; only to a select few. But those select few are then given two distinct privileges. First, whereas for equitable assignment the original creditor should (normally) be joined to the action to recover the debt, for negotiable instruments that is not required; whoever possesses the document holds the right and can bring the action. Second, 'negotiability' means that the recipient of the instrument who takes it in good faith (that is, without notice of any defects in the transferor's title) and for value (that is, in exchange for something else) is given a *clean* title to the instrument. That is much better than receiving the transferor's title to the debt because that existing title could, of course, have unknown or unknowable defects.

In contrast, assignment in equity does not confer a clean title, giving rise to a number of issues discussed in chapter four. Lord Mansfield explained the commercial significance of clean title when he extended negotiability to bank notes in *Miller v Race* (1758) 1 Burr 452: the removal of any risk of defects by clean title means that parties can have confidence in the face value of the instrument and enable it to be given 'the currency and credit of money' (see also pages 11–12 above). In other words, the common law created clean title to facilitate the commercial use of these debt obligations as liquid assets and as payment mechanisms for other debts.

With the rise of bank money, electronic payment systems and the modern securities markets, negotiable instruments have lost much of their importance in commerce. Modern commercial parties have not sought to persuade the courts to extend negotiability to these new ways of trading debts. The reason for this, probably, is that only equity can effectively trace through bank accounts, so defects in title in modern banking and securities system are likely to arise only in equity. The same is true for modern securities structures because they are put into effect using trust and sub-trust structures (Gullifer 2022, 255). Equitable interests cannot be asserted against a subsequent good faith purchaser for value. Because this is the same test as to create a clean title over a negotiable instrument, it gives commercial parties the equivalent level of confidence in respect of bank money and intermediated securities as historically they had with negotiable instruments.

TWO MODELS OF EQUITABLE ASSIGNMENT

The operation of assignment of debts in equity is less straightforward, although it is clear enough that it is nothing like negotiability at common law. There are two different ways of understanding equitable assignment.

(1) *The trust model.* This model starts from the proposition that nothing is *transferred*; the right to payment at law remains with assignor. Rather, by the assignment, a *new* equitable right in respect of the existing debt vests in the assignee to create a bare trust (see, for example, McFarlane and Stevens 2010; Edelman and Elliott 2015; Tham 2019). This reflects the historical development of assignment out of the law of trusts. It also provides a substantive justification for the rule that the assignor must be joined to any action brought by the assignee against the debtor. On the trust analysis, this resembles the '*Vandepitte* procedure', named after *Vandepitte v Preferred Accident Insurance Corpn of New York* [1933] AC 70, whereby the beneficiary under a trust can sue a third party if the trustee is joined to the action.

(2) *The transfer model.* Here, equitable assignment instead means 'the immediate transfer of an existing proprietary right ... from the assignor to the assignee': *Norman v Federal Comr of Taxation* (1963) 109 CLR 9, 26 (per Windeyer J). This is now the dominant model in the common law, as is evident from the decision in *National Westminster Bank plc v Kapoor* [2012] 1 All ER 1201. In that case, at [30], Etherton LJ held that joinder of the assignor to the action of the assignee against the debtor was 'purely a procedural requirement and can be dispensed with' where appropriate (that is, where it is not felt necessary, for whatever reason, to bind the assignor to the judgment). That decision creates a substantive difference between the equitable assignee of a debt and the position of a beneficiary under a trust of a debt, who must join the trustee in the *Vandepitte* procedure to sue on the debt as a matter of substantive law.

Notwithstanding *Kapoor*, the transfer model still faces a particular problem, which is that a contractual debt is a chose of action *at common law*, and so cannot itself be transferred or enforced *in equity*. For equity to have any effect at all it necessarily has to create an equitable interest in the debt, and then enforce that interest. Advocates of the transfer model struggle to accommodate this point. Tolhurst 2016, 39–42, gives transfer an 'extended meaning' to encompass the creation of new rights in equity on the basis that that constitutes, in functional terms, a transfer. But that merely demonstrates that notion of a transfer is inaccurate: the separation of legal and beneficial interests, by definition, means no rights have actually passed from assignor to assignee; rather, a trust has been created. Smith and Leslie 2018, 231–32 accept the proposition that a bare trust arises in these circumstances but nonetheless maintain their preference for describing this as an (attempted) transfer. They make a number of arguments (246–49), most of which boil down to the point that the transfer model has been dominant for a considerable period of time. But that amounts to a *description* of the law rather than an *explanation* for it. Smith and Leslie also point out that the transfer model is the basis on which Parliament has intervened by statute. That is admittedly more difficult, and we turn to this next.

TRADING DEBTS BY STATUTORY ASSIGNMENT

Since Stuart times Parliament has intervened on occasion in favour of the continuing commodification of debts. That policy was to be expected.

The transformation of debt into property led to cheaper credit, and more of it too. Indeed, the Crown itself was a direct and significant beneficiary of the growing commercial practice of dealing in debts. In particular, the state had found it much easier to borrow money to fund its wars and other projects after the financial revolution that began in the reign of William and Mary and the foundation of the Bank of England. A secondary market grew up which allowed creditors to buy and sell government bonds freely, making them a more attractive proposition to buy when issued via the Bank of England in the first place. The success of the secondary market in state debt in turn encouraged the further development of secondary markets in private commercial debt. Indeed, it was during this period that the City of London became a leading global centre for financial activity, and a powerful lobby group at Westminster.

We have already seen that Parliament intervened in 1704 to reverse Holt CJ's decision in *Clerke v Martin* which had attracted the horror of the City. Another objection to the trade of debts was removed in 1867, when Parliament largely abolished debtors' prisons – although it is fair to say that this reform was driven by social reformers rather than financiers in the square mile.

The most significant intervention came only a few years later. By the Judicature Acts of 1873 and 1875, the systems of law and equity were brought into a single Court system. While this was primarily a fusion of the administration of these two systems of law, limited steps were taken in s 25 of the 1873 Act to remove some of the substantive differences between common law and equity as well. Section 25(6) concerned the assignment of debts. The provision is now found in s 136 of the Law of Property Act 1925. It relevantly provides:

> Any absolute assignment by writing under the hand of the assignor (not purporting to be by way of charge only) of any debt or other legal thing in action, of which express notice in writing has been given to the debtor, trustee or other person from whom the assignor would have been entitled to claim such debt or thing in action, is effectual in law (subject to equities having priority over the right of the assignee) to pass and transfer from the date of such notice (a) the legal right to such debt or thing in action; (b) all legal and other remedies for the same; and (c) the power to give a good discharge for the same without the concurrence of the assignor.

As can be seen, statutory assignment has additional formality requirements to assignment in equity. As well as the three Certainties, the assignment must be (i) in writing, (ii) signed by the assignor and (iii) notified in writing to the debtor. Such formalities in private law are said to have three functions (Fuller 1941, 800–01): *first*, an evidentiary function, providing evidence of the existence of the thing in issue; *second*, a cautionary function, encouraging parties to stop and think before binding themselves; and *third*, a channelling function, providing 'a simple and external test of enforceability'.

Three concurrent formalities might be thought excessive; one or two might fulfil these functions just as well. Law reformers in New Zealand – which inherited s 25(6) of the Judicature Act 1873 – certainly thought so: it abolished notice as a precondition for a valid statutory assignment in 2007. However, that may not have been the best formality to abolish, given notice remains central to the question of priorities between competing assignments and protects against some forms of set-off (as discussed further in chapter four). Signature would have made much more sense as a candidate for abolition.

Section 25(6), now s 136, expressly characterises assignment as a 'transfer'. Judges in the wake of the 1873 Act took the view that the provision was merely intended to speed up the procedural aspects of a claim brought by an assignee, and it was not intended to create a new type of assignment different from equity: see, for example, *Re Westerton* [1919] 2 Ch 104, 133 (Sargant J). That construction is supported not only by the context in which s 25(6) was drafted (that is, administrative but not substantive fusion of law and equity), but also because the provision does not itself define assignment, which suggests the draftsman was building on the judge-made concept rather than departing from it (Turner 2008, 318 and 329). If that is right, the language of 'transfer' in the 1873 Act might be taken as evidence that the transfer model of equitable assignment was well established by the mid-Victorian period (Smith and Leslie 2018, 222 and 246).

The better view, however, is that the statute creates a *different* type of assignment, and so the 'transfer' model adopted the statute cannot simply be 'read across' to equitable assignment. The three major differences are as follows.

First, as we have already seen, there are formal preconditions for statutory assignment which are additional to the three Certainties required whenever there are dealings in property. If the draftsman had simply intended to simplify the mechanics of an assignee bringing a claim, these formalities would not have been added. Their inclusion suggests that Parliament was intending to do something new by s 25(6), rather than simply put assignment in equity on a statutory footing. Indeed, had Parliament had intended that the principles of assignment in equity should be adopted in preference to the common law position, it would either have said so expressly, or would not have said anything at all and instead left matters to s 25(11) by which, if 'there is any conflict or variance between the Rules of Equity and the Rules of the Common Law with reference to the same matter, the Rules of Equity shall prevail'.

Second, the scope of statutory assignment is narrower than equitable assignment. Equity will assign equitable choses in action, will respond to conditional assignments, and will assign part of a debt. The latter two are not possible by s 136; the former ought not to be possible on a fair reading of the language of the provision, albeit the courts have adopted a strained interpretation: contrast *Re Pain* [1919] 1 Ch 38, 44 (per Younger J). Moreover, an agreement to assign a future debt or an existing debt in the future will, if supported by valuable consideration, take effect in equity *automatically* at the required time. This is the same doctrine as gives automatic effect to security over future debts, which will be discussed in chapter six. Statutory assignment cannot be used in the same way. The act of assignment will only be valid if it purports to make an *immediate* transfer of an existing debt.

Third, s 136 prescribes different consequences on assignment to equity. One way of describing this is that the requirements of equitable assignment *and* the additional formal requirements of the provision are satisfied, the trust effects of equitable assignment are overridden and the entitlements set out at (a)–(c) of the statutory provision are transferred away from the assignor to the assignee: Tham 2019, 327–29. The result is that the assignor no longer needs to be joined to any action by the assignee against the debtor; the assignee can instead sue in their own name. We have seen that some judges and commentators consider this to be a purely procedural point, but in fact this represents a substantive distinction. It reflects the fact that, rather than operating by way of a trust, 'the debt is transferred to the assignee and becomes as though it had been his from the beginning; it is no longer to be the debt of the assignor at all': *Read v Brown* (1888) 22 QBD 128, 132 (per Lord Esher MR) (but contrast Tham 2019, 352–55).

4. TRADE IN SERVICES

Trade in services is commercially more important in many developed economies than in goods, including the UK, but is legally less complicated, at least for the purposes of this chapter. Services can be divided into two. First, there are services which result in an 'end product', that is, some new asset. The principles already considered in this chapter apply to determine when title to that end product is transferred to the buyer. Other services constitute 'pure services'. An example would be the advice rendered by large professional firms (lawyers, accountants, management consultants and so on) to commercial parties. Although there may well be confidentiality in such professional advice, there are no property rights in it, and so the conceptual complications considered earlier in this chapter in respect of the transfer of title does not arise. Of course, the services must be rendered as promised. But the possibility that they will not be so rendered is a question of performance risk, which is addressed separately in chapter five.

5. TRADE IN CREDIT

A good way of understanding financial transactions – as opposed to transactions for goods and services – is that they are about trade *in* credit risk, rather than being trade for something that simply gives rise to credit risk (Benjamin 2007).

Trading in credit typically involves a 'funded' position, that is, the provision of capital by one party to another. For these purposes, we are not concerned with equity investment, where a commercial enterprise raises new funds from shareholders (if a company) or partners (if a partnership). That is a question about the *internal* workings of companies and partnerships. Provision of capital by way of debt, however, is a way that a commercial enterprise can raise funds from *external* commercial counterparties. In debt finance, capital is usually lent in exchange for a fee – usually in the form of interest – representing a combination of the credit risk being taken together with the time value of money.

Debt finance can simply be through the extension of 'trade credit', which arises where a seller or provider of services does not require payment at the very same time as providing the goods or services in question. The debts then owed are often called 'book debts'. However, debt finance is also associated with formal lending by financial institutions. A bank – or group of banks, called a 'syndicate' – may, for example, lend a company a sum of money for a stipulated term or provide an overdraft facility, in exchange for repayment of both capital and interest. Debt finance can also take many other forms. For example, commercial enterprises can raise debt finance by 'debt securities', also known as bonds or notes: tradeable debt instruments that may be held by numerous investors. These were originally issued in the form of physical documents and could be traded as such through the doctrine of negotiability. However, nowadays securities are nearly always 'dematerialised' and held through professional intermediaries for efficiency of trading on the modern markets (see page 36 above).

Asset-backed financial transactions are those which 'earmark' certain assets for repayment. A borrower will often provide security or some functional equivalent (such buying goods on credit on RoT terms), something discussed further in chapter six. Another example is 'factoring', also known as 'receivables financing', which we will also discuss in chapter five. Capital is provided to a company which, in return, assigns what is, and will be, owed to it by trade debtors. This is often used to give the company a steady income stream, rather than being dependent on when trade debtors pay their debts for goods and services provided to them. The equivalent of interest is generated by the discount applied to the debts assigned under the arrangement. This is a common form of financing for smaller businesses, who may lack assets other than book debts to offer to lenders to encourage them to lend or to lend at a lower cost, given unsecured lending often attracts higher – and not infrequently very high – interest rates.

Not all financial trading involves funded positions. 'Simple' financial trading includes guarantees, insurance, derivatives, and letters of credits. All of these transactions also involve the one party taking the credit risk of the other party, that is, the risk that they will not, or cannot, pay as promised, but *without* first advancing capital. Parties may trade in these financial products for purely speculative, profit-making reasons but there are at least two other good reasons for these types of transactions (Benjamin 2007, 86–88).

First, they can themselves provide a form of defence against credit risk. If, for instance, a bank lends to a company, it may want to mitigate that credit risk by having the option of also taking the credit risk of a third party: the loan could be guaranteed by a director or parent company, or the default could be insured, or subject to a credit default swap. Likewise, as we saw earlier in this chapter (at page 14 above), letters of credits are used by sellers to mitigate the credit risk posed by buyers in international trade.

Second, they can be used to hedge against other risks. So, for example, a business may wish to protect against the prospect of rising interest rates or energy or commodity prices, and so take out a future or swap for a fee. Protection from loss can also be secured through insurance, paying what is called a 'premium'. For example, a business might insure against the risk of a loss of assets in an accident or a war or due to sanctions or insure its profits against the occurrence of possible future events such as the closure due to the outbreak of a disease such as COVID-19. In this way, financial law can translate risks *of any kind* into monetary value, and so make it into credit risk, that can then be traded like any other commodity between counterparties.

3

Transacting

In this chapter we move from *what* commercial parties do to *how* they do it. For a commercial economy to be comprised of anything other than sole traders running rudimentary businesses, rules are needed by which commercial enterprises can transact – do deals – through other people. The need for rules is even more pronounced in modern commercial life, where most business is now done through corporate entities. Companies are legal creations which can only act via human intermediaries. A rule-book is needed for when this can happen. As Lord Hoffmann explained in *Meridian Global Funds Management Asia Ltd v Securities Commission* [1995] AC 500, at 506:

> Any proposition about a company necessarily involves a reference to a set of rules. A company exists because there is a rule (usually in a statute) which says that a *persona ficta* shall be deemed to exist and to have certain of the powers, rights and duties of a natural person. But there would be little sense in deeming such a *persona ficta* to exist unless there were also rules to tell one what acts were to count as acts of the company.

These rules are known as the law of agency. Agents have the power to change the rights and duties of their principals. Agency is the lifeblood of modern commercial law: almost every commercial transaction and every commercial dispute will involve the law of agency in some way. The controversial part of the law of agency is therefore not so much its existence as its *extent*. The rules have to limit the power of the agent to affect the principal's legal position to protect the principal's autonomy, otherwise principals would be slaves to their agents.

Two ideas are explored in this chapter. The *first* is that the law of agency is not susceptible to a single justification: different rules are underpinned by different rationales. In particular, an agent's authority to transact is not a response to a single event. Rather, there are four different scenarios in which it can arise: (i) by an objective agreement between principal and agent, (ii) by an objective agreement between principal and third party, (iii) by estoppel and (iv) by statute. While these are four different events, as will be seen, (ii) and (iii) can also be considered as derivative of (i). Even though there is no unifying principle underpinning the law of agency, and some aspects of agency can be explained better by reference to other parts of private law (such as contract law), agents should still be regarded an as independent ('*sui generis*' to use the old language) phenomenon in law. This is the *second* idea in this chapter. Contrary to the arguments of agency sceptics, the law of agency cannot, and should not, be overlooked as a distinct conceptual underpinning of commercial law. Most obviously, in the context of transacting, the paradigm case involves actual authority stemming from an agreement between principal and agent, and that paradigm also provides the foundation for apparent authority and estoppel too. As this chapter explains, the law endows that agreement with special properties which cannot be re-explained in purely contractual terms.

1. THE POWERS OF AGENCY

Agency is concerned with the conferral of 'a legal power on an agent to alter his principal's legal relationships with third persons' with the principal 'under a correlative liability to have his legal relations altered' (Dowrick 1954, 36). But the language of 'affecting legal relations' is a little vague. It is more accurate to say that agency allows the principal to exercise its own powers through another person (Leow 2019, 114).

The capacity of agents to exercise their principals' powers is considerable. Agents are appointed to transact on behalf of their principals with third parties, but they may bind their principals to transactions they did not necessarily want or expect. Moreover, their actions can also lead to those transactions being corrected or reversed. Principals may also find themselves treated as though their agents' wrongdoing is attributed to them, or at least held responsible for that wrongdoing. While the heart of this chapter is concerned with the rules on transacting, we first need to sketch out this broader picture in order to get a proper sense of what agency is all about.

TRANSACTING

Agents are typically appointed to enter into and perform contracts on behalf of their principals. The rules which empower and limit the ability of agents to bind their principals to contracts with third parties are traditionally described using the language of 'authority': actual authority, apparent or ostensible authority, usual authority and so on. Similar 'authority' rules exist for dealings in property. There, the general rule is that a principal is bound by an agent's receipt and transfer of interests in property so long as those transactions are within the scope of the agent's actual or apparent authority, ratified by the principal, or where the principal has empowered the agent to hold himself out as the 'apparent owner' of the property.

We examine these rules on authority later in this chapter. Suffice it at this stage to note that the names given to these types of authority contain normative assertions about the basis on which the principal becomes party to the transaction made by the agent. Thus 'actual' authority hints that the agent has been conferred with a real authority; in contrast, 'apparent' authority suggests it is not real but a façade, which nonetheless can have legal consequences; and 'ratification' is real authority conferred after the event, when a contract was originally concluded in the absence of authority. On this view, actual authority is the foundation of agency, with other forms of authority extending its effects in different ways. As we shall see, this account of agency and authority has much to commend it.

Authority is one way in which an act of an agent is attributed to a principal. In *Meridian Global Funds*, at 506–07, Lord Hoffmann divided the rules of attribution into 'primary', 'general' and 'special' rules. We will come back to 'special' rules shortly because these are only relevant in cases where a principal is said to be liable for an agent's wrongdoing. The other two categories are relevant in cases of transacting (and also correcting and reversing transactions). They are simply another way of dividing up scenarios where actual and apparent authority has been conferred on an agent for a company. Primary rules of attribution respond to the company's constitution. This is the source for the initial conferral of actual authority by a company. It is necessary in circumstances where the principal is not a human being that can do this for him or herself. (The board of directors and any other agents initially authorised by the law in turn can confer authority on sub-agents, and sub-sub-agents and so on, until there are chains of authority radiating out from the company's board of directors.) General attribution rules in the corporate context refer to the authorisation of individuals directly or indirectly by the board, as well as recognising the fact that the company can also be bound by those acting with apparent authority. Of course, where the principal is a human being, there is no need for the 'primary' rules of attribution; the general attribution rules can also apply to the initial conferral of actual authority.

Many agents are not given, and are not held out to have, authority to contract or deal in property for their principals. Their authority is confined to representing their principals in some more limited way, such as making introductions, negotiating deals to be approved by their principals or communicating decisions made by their principals. These types of agent are typically depicted in melancholy terms as 'incomplete agents'. This might be questioned in practice and as a matter of principle. First, it suggests that these 'representative agents' are unusual, whereas in fact they are commonplace in commercial transactions. Introducing agents, for example, are central to the functioning of a number of markets such as real estate (few estate agents are authorised to sell the property they market) as well as providing access to particular markets, where business is dependent on the quality of the agent's contacts. Moreover, it suggests that these agents are not true agents, whereas in fact they are perfectly capable of affecting the legal position of their principals, as we shall see next (see also pages 68–69 below on 'communicating agents').

CORRECTING AND REVERSING TRANSACTIONS

Contracts can be rectified or rescinded. The reason for this often rests with the conduct and knowledge of agents, no matter whether they are 'complete' or 'incomplete' agents. The basic rule is that, where agents are transacting for their principals in the scope of their actual or apparent authority, their acts and their states of mind when so acting are 'attributed' to the company.

For example, the documented terms of contracts may be corrected if, by mistake, what is written down does not reflect the real agreement. If the contract is concluded by an agent, it is the agent's mistake which counts. Where the agent merely negotiated the contract for agreement by the principal, the negotiator's mistake might count if it can be shown that the negotiator was 'really' the decision-maker despite his lack of authority to conclude the contract, because the principal would typically accept his recommendation (Davies 2020). In either case, we say that the mistake is 'attributed' to the principal. Rescission works in the same way. So, for example, if the agent concluding the contract or acting as the relevant decision-maker was relying on a lie or induced by a threat, then the rules of attribution are engaged and the principal can set the contract aside for misrepresentation or duress. And if that agent made the misrepresentation or the threat, or was on notice of it, then the principal may find that the third party can set aside the contract because the actions or knowledge of the agent is attributed to the principal.

The same principles of attribution are applied when non-contractual transactions are reversed. Suppose, for example, that the principal makes payment by reason of an agent's mistake and then seeks to recover the money by an action in unjust enrichment. In modern commercial organisations, attributing mistakes can be a complex task. In *BP Oil International Ltd v Target Shipping Ltd* [2012] EWHC 1590 (Comm), the claimant was over-charged freight on a charterparty. The invoice was approved by two employees and then processed by two other employees. A fifth employee in a sister company (correctly) thought the freight was not due but did not say anything. The fifth employee clearly was not mistaken. Nor could it be said that the two 'processing' employees were acting by mistake: they correctly reacted to the approval of the payments. But first two 'approving' employees were mistaken. They had erroneously believed that all the freight was due and should be paid. They were acting in the scope of their authority when, on that mistaken basis, they had approved payment. Andrew Smith J held that this sufficed to allow the principal to bring a claim in mistake, despite the knowledge to the contrary of the fifth employee. That was because the fifth employee had not intervened in the approval procedure and so was not a relevant decision-maker; it would have been different had he involved himself in the payment process, rather than keeping his thoughts to himself.

WRONGDOING

So far, we have been considering transactions. But rules of attribution also allow an agent's wrongdoing to be attributed to the principal. Where the attribution rules are satisfied, the principal is treated as having committed the relevant wrong itself. This is the only way in which principals can be liable for the crimes of their agents. But it is also one way in which principals can be liable for the torts of their agents, the other being vicarious liability.

(1) *Attributing wrongs.* Attribution rules have always been different for criminal wrongdoing. Historically only the mens rea of the 'directing mind or will' of the company could be attributed to the company: *Tesco Supermarkets Ltd* v *Nattrass* [1972] AC 152. In *Global Meridian Funds*, however, Lord Hoffmann emphasised this 'special' rule of attribution (at 507, original emphasis):

> the court must fashion a special rule of attribution for the particular substantive rule. This is always a matter of interpretation: given that it was intended to apply to a company, how was it intended to apply? Whose act (or knowledge, or state of mind) was *for this purpose* intended to count as the act etc. of the company? One finds the answer to this question by applying the usual canons of interpretation, taking into account the language of the rule (if it is a statute) and its content and policy.

This must be right. Principles of actual and apparent authority were developed to deal with concluding, correcting and reversing transactions. It would be wrong to apply those without further thought to the criminal law. It is much more principled instead to ask what attribution rule is appropriate for the particular offence in question.

The same point can made for civil wrongdoing. Traditionally, however, the courts started by asking whether the agent was authorised to commit the wrongdoing when considering whether to attribute it to the principal, before then asking whether any exception ought to be applied. In *Bilta (UK) Ltd (In Liquidation)* v *Nazir* [2016] AC 1, that two-stage process was swept away for a single contextual approach. Lords Toulson and Hodge held that (at [191]): 'the "legal context", that is, the nature and subject matter of the relevant rule and duty, is always relevant' when considering whether a wrongful act or state of mind of an individual should be attributed to a company. In that case, it was not open to former directors to attribute their unlawful conduct to the company in the context of the company bringing breach of duty claims against the directors. Lord Toulson and Lord Hodge reasoned that attributing the directors' conduct to the company and thereby barring its claim would negate the very existence of the directors' duties.

The legal context of the claim is equally important when a company sues a third party who is not a director or other agent, but where the wrongdoing of an agent of the company remains in some way relevant. For example, where the claim is that the third party was an accessory or conspirator to a breach by an agent of the company, the agent's breach should not be attributed to the company. On the other hand, where the company's claim is against an auditor who has negligently failed to catch a director's fraudulent activities, or against an insurer in circumstances where a company agent has failed to disclose a material fact, it may well be that the wrongdoing should be attributed to the company. Whereas in the former case, the company can fairly be considered the victim of the wrong; in the latter cases, the victims are shareholders, creditors or other third parties, from whose perspective the company itself is the wrongdoer.

(2) *Attributing responsibility for wrongdoing.* Vicarious liability operates differently to the rules of attribution we have just been considering. In attribution cases, the principal is taken to have acted directly or personally but for vicarious liability, it is *responsibility* for the wrongdoing, and not the wrongdoing *itself*, which is attributed to the principal. Vicarious liability was developed in a series of judgments given by Sir John Holt as Lord Chief Justice in late seventeenth-century England. That development ran alongside the emergence of a commercial economy and more sophisticated commercial enterprises, and the consequent increasing use of agents. The greater the use of agents, the more numerous the instances of agent wrongdoing, and the more the court had to grapple with whether and when a principal should be responsible for an agent's wrong.

Holt CJ developed vicarious liability by asking whether the tortfeasor was an agent and what authority they had (see further Ibbetson 1999, 181–82; Giliker 2010, 12–13). In the modern law, there is a two-stage test for vicarious liability, which still owes much to Holt CJ's original approach.

First, the person alleged to be vicariously liable must be in a relevant relationship with the person who has actually committed the wrong. It is well-established that an agency relationship counts at this first stage; indeed, that was the historical basis for this doctrine. However, regrettably, the modern approach in England distracts from this by asking whether the tortfeasor and defendant were in a relationship of employment or 'akin' to employment, whilst at the same time insisting that a defendant can never be liable for the torts of an 'independent contractor': see, for example, *Various Claimants v Barclays Bank plc* [2020] AC 973. It would

be much more straightforward to ask whether the tortfeasor was authorised to act for or represent the defendant in some way, even if only as
an 'incomplete' agent. Indeed, that explains why independent contractors
are excluded because they carry out their work 'not as a representative
but as a principal': *Colonial Mutual Life Assurance Society Ltd v Producers
& Citizens Co-operative Assurance Company of Australia Ltd* (1931) 46
CLR 41, 48–49 (Dixon J). That approach attracted the support of distinguished US jurists (for example, Holmes 1891–92, 14–16) and has
found favour in New Zealand (*Nathan v Dollar & Sense Finance Ltd*
[2008] 2 NZLR 557). However, it has been rejected in Australia despite
the valiant efforts of McHugh J (see, for example, *Hollis v Vabu Pty Ltd*
(2001) 207 CLR 41) and, while the point has not been tested in English
law, the 'akin to employment' test is now probably too well-established to
be overturned.

Second, the agent's wrong must be connected to their relationship
with their principal. Sometimes an agent will have been instructed by
the principal to commit the wrong. But very often that is not the case,
and some mechanism is needed to work out where to draw the line. Until
relatively recently, the test at the second stage was expressed in terms
of agency and authority. This was largely derived from Holt CJ's early
decisions but became known as the 'Salmond test' (Salmond 1907, 83).
It asked whether the wrong was: 'either (1) a wrongful act authorised by
the master, or (2) a wrongful and unauthorised mode of doing some act
authorised by the master'.

The problem with this test was that principles of actual and apparent
authority were developed as principles governing when a principal
is bound by an agent's transacting. It did not make sense to use them
to determine whether the principal should take responsibility for the
wrongdoing of the agent, because different considerations are in play.
Indeed, for this reason, the case law on vicarious liability rapidly began
to use authority in a more attenuated way than in cases of transacting. So
the same word – 'authority' – began to mean different things in the two
different contexts.

Fortunately, the Salmond test has now been abandoned in favour of a
new 'close connection' test, emanating from the decisions of the Supreme
Court of Canada in *Bazley v Curry* (1999) 174 CLR (4th) 71 and *Jacobi v
Griffiths* (1999) 174 DLR (4th) 71. The test now applied is that:

> the wrongful conduct must be so closely connected with acts the [agent] was
> authorised to do that, for the purpose of the liability of the [principal] to third

parties, the wrongful conduct may fairly and properly be regarded as done by the [agent] while acting in the ordinary course of the [principal's] business or the [agent's] employment: *Dubai Aluminium Co Ltd v Salaam* [2003] 2 AC 366, at [23] (per Lord Nicholls).

It can be seen from this formulation that authority is still relevant as a starting point, but it is not determinative in the same way as the Salmond test. While criticisms can be made of the uncertainties inherent in the new test, the diminished role for authority must be right. One happy consequence of this is that the law can now adopt a uniform approach to what is meant by authority both in contract and in tort.

The prevailing, and most persuasive, justification for vicarious liability is 'enterprise risk'. The principal takes the benefit of transacting by agency and, as a matter of fairness, must also take the burden of responsibility for risks of wrongdoing created by that agency. As Lord Nicholls explained in *Dubai Aluminium* at [21]:

> The underlying legal policy is based on the recognition that carrying on a business enterprise necessarily involves risks to others. It involves the risk that others will be harmed by wrongful acts committed by the agents through whom the business is carried on. When those risks ripen into loss, it is just that the business should be responsible for compensating the person who has been wronged.

This is certainly preferable to the various other policy justifications found in the literature for vicarious liability (for example, deep pockets, loss spreading, relative blame and deterrence) which cannot easily be reconciled with most of the rest of tort law. Some argue that vicarious liability recognises where the principal has committed the wrong itself (see Stevens 2007, 257–74). But the problem with this 'master's tort' theory is that it conflates the distinction discussed above between attributing wrongdoing and responsibility for wrongdoing.

CHECKS AND BALANCES

Given the power an agent can wield in relation to a principal's affairs, the law has developed various checks and balances on its exercise. First and foremost, the agent must act in the best interests of the principal and is a fiduciary of the principal. Fiduciary duties mean that, unless otherwise permitted by the principal, the agent must exercise authority to transact free from conflicts of interest and must not make any profit from the agency.

The imposition of these fiduciary duties is the necessary response to the principal granting the power to transact to the agent, and thereby giving that person control over its autonomy. It is inherent in granting this power to the agent that it must be exercised loyally for the principal (Smith 2014, 612–20). But fiduciary duties are not the only check on the agency's actions. For example, the agent also owes the principal duties of care and confidentiality, must follow instructions when they are given, and give an account of the transactions entered into if requested by the principal. Further, when something goes wrong, and the principal is liable for what the agent has done, the agent is liable to indemnify the principal for that liability.

While the agent does not have the same power over third parties, third parties nevertheless are vulnerable to the conduct of agents, and therefore are also afforded protection. Third parties can, of course, conclude the contract on terms that the agent is liable on it in addition to the principal. This involves an exercise in contractual construction, aided by a series of presumptions developed against the agent by the courts out of concern to protect the third party. Further, if an agent commits a wrong, the agent remains liable to the third party in addition to making the principal liable. And where a third party has a claim in unjust enrichment against the principal, in some circumstances it may also have a claim against the agent, although this is subject to some controversy. Space precludes further discussion here (see instead Burrows 2012, 558–68). These various rules have the common feature of preventing the agent from 'dropping out' in all circumstances, thereby giving the third party two people against whom they can enforce their remedies. This is valuable because the agent may represent a preferable credit risk to the principal.

The most significant protection given to a third party against an agent's conduct is probably the claim for damages for breach of warranty of authority against the agent. This claim arises if it turns out that the agent did not have power to transact on behalf the principal. The third party is entitled to compensation to put it in the position it would have been in if the warranty had been true and the agent had in fact bound the principal to the contract. It does not matter that the agent innocently misrepresented their authority, so breach of warranty of authority cannot be explained away as an example of the tort of deceit. Moreover, because it precedes *Hedley Byrne & Co Ltd v Heller & Partners Ltd* [1964] AC 465, it also cannot be explained as a claim for economic loss arising from negligent misstatement. In Victorian England, the judges instead had to rationalise the action as arising from a collateral contract, by which the agent promises the third party he has authority in consideration for which the third party enters into the transaction: *Collen v Wright* (1857) 7 E&B 647. As a result, the liability is strict. There are three elements to the claim.

First, the purported agent must have represented that they (or another agent) had authority to bind a particular principal. This is readily implied from the circumstances in which a disclosed agent is dealing with a third party. It is often said that the doctrine does not extend to representations as to the principal's willingness to perform the contract or the principal's solvency, but this is a default rule and there is nothing stopping the agent from making those representations expressly.

Second, the agent must not have authority to act for the principal in question. There is a debate about whether the action arises whenever the agent lacks actual authority, or whether other forms of authority will do (see, for example, Reynolds 2012, 201). It would be an odd thing for an agent to have represented that he did not have actual authority but merely apparent authority, or that his actions would be ratified despite being unauthorised, so it is probably correct to say that there is a breach in every case where there is no actual authority. However, the point is unlikely ever to be tested: even if liability technically arises where the agent did not have actual authority, the existence of another form of authority (for example, apparent authority) means that the principal is bound, so there is no loss and thus no point in bringing a damages claim.

Third, but for the representation, the third party would not have entered into the transaction: *Firbank's Executors v Humphreys* (1886) 18 QBD 54, 60 (per Lord Esher MR). This causation requirement means that the third party cannot have known about the lack of authority at the time: *Halbot v Lens* [1901] 1 Ch 344. If the third party knew about the lack of authority and proceeded to transact anyway, the representation cannot have caused the conclusion of the transaction.

The protection for third parties provided by breach of warranty of authority is anomalous and excessive. It is highly likely that this doctrine is something of a historic artefact. If *Hedley Byrne* had been decided 100 or so years earlier, there would never have been a need to (somewhat artificially) rationalise the doctrine as turning on an implied collateral contract and thereby impose strict liability. As developed, the doctrine means that an agent can be liable even if it has acted honestly and even if the third party – had it taken due care – could have found out the true position.

It might be pointed out in response that, since the doctrine is based on an agent's implied representation, it is always open to the agent to qualify or displace its liability at the outset. But that puts matters the wrong way around: if third parties want this protection, they should have to bargain (and pay) for it.

There are various oven-ready options that could be used to reform the doctrine. The drafters of the UNIDROIT Principles of International Commercial Contracts 2004 proposed that the doctrine does not apply if the third party ought reasonably to have known about the lack of authority (see article 2.2.6). Other international commercial codes (discussed in Reynolds 2012, 195) take a similar approach. In domestic law, the Powers of Attorney Act 1971, s 5(1) relieves agents of liability for innocent mis-statements as to the continuing validity of powers of attorney: the misstatement must be negligent or fraudulent. It would be sensible to widen that statutory exception to protect all innocent agents who have otherwise breached their warranty of authority.

2. THE AUTHORITY OF AGENTS

Having sketched out the broad landscape of the law of agency, we can now focus on transacting and, in particular, the rules of authority which permit agents to contract and otherwise transact on behalf of principals. The language of 'authority' has been criticised as confused and confusing (Seavey 1920, 860–61), and so it is important to be clear at the outset as to the definition used in this chapter. Authority here means those powers by which one person (the 'agent') can bind another (the 'principal') in a contract or other transaction with someone else (the 'third party') and perform the principal's obligations, or exercise the principal's rights, under those transactions. As we shall see, there are a number of powers answering that definition.

ACTUAL AUTHORITY

Actual authority arises from an agreement between agent and principal that the agent can transact for the principal. The agreement can be express or implied, and the test for the existence and scope of such an agreement is objective. Diplock LJ famously said that the express terms of a mandate are to be construed 'by applying the ordinary principles of construction of contracts' (*Freeman & Lockyer (A Firm) v Buckhurst Park Properties (Mangal) Ltd* [1964] 2 QB 480, 502), although a more textual approach prevails where authority is conferred by deed.

There is a special defence to a breach of mandate claim that applies where the terms of the instruction are ambiguous; the agent is not taken to be in breach if he has acted in good faith on a reasonable, albeit incorrect, understanding of those instructions: *Ireland v Livingston* (1871–72) LR 5 HL 395. The *Ireland* exception was developed for pragmatic reasons before modern forms of communication and will rarely apply today, given how easy (and thus reasonable) it is now for agents to clarify ambiguous instructions: *European Asian Bank AG v Punjab & Sind Bank (No 2)* [1983] 1 WLR 642, 656 (per Goff LJ).

IMPLIED ACTUAL AUTHORITY

In contract law, implied terms are divided into terms implied in fact, by law and by custom. For agency law, however, the cat is typically skinned a slightly different way. Implied actual authority is divided into *four* categories. These are in fact referable back to the more familiar three categories seen in contract law:

(1) *Authority implied from conduct or circumstances.* An example of this first kind of authority is where a company board designates one of their number 'managing director', thereby implicitly giving him greater authority than the non-executive directors to deal with the day-to-day business of the company: *Hely-Hutchinson v Brayhead Ltd* [1968] 1 QB 549 (CA) 583–84 (per Lord Denning MR). This can probably be explained on the basis of the 'officious bystander' test: if a passer-by had asked reasonable people in the position of the board members whether they thereby intended to confer greater authority on the managing director to transact on behalf of the company, they would have testily responded: 'Of course!'.

(2) *Usual implied authority.* Agents often act in the course of an established trade, profession or businesses such as (to name but a few) auctioneers, estate agents, stockbrokers, shopfloor workers, company

executives and lawyers. Subject to the express terms of their engagement, authority is implicitly conferred and limited by the fact that the agent has been engaged to act in the course of the established occupation in question. So, for example, auctioneers are conferred with authority to contract on behalf of both buyer and seller, whereas estate agents are not authorised to do more than market a property and accept bids to take back to the seller. This is the 'usual' scope of what these types of agents are allowed to do, and so, unless the principal expressly says otherwise, they are always implicitly conferred with that authority on appointment. In some cases, the analysis might be that the authority is implied by law; in other cases, it might be safer to resort again to the officious bystander test.

(3) *Customary implied authority.* In contracts, terms are implied by custom of the relevant market, trade or business if (i) certain (ii) well-known and (iii) reasonable, or, if not reasonable, brought to the actual notice of the principal. The same test can be used to imply actual authority. Until early nineteenth century, this was a well-used technique for moulding commercial law to commercial practice. Some judges – most famously Holt CJ and Lord Mansfield – even assembled special juries of merchants to hear cases involving issues of mercantile custom. Nowadays, however, it is very difficult to establish new customs. That is because commercial life is increasingly concerned with the hands of bigger commercial parties who deal on standard terms which leave no room for the unspoken customary practice. As a result, this third type of implied actual authority is now the least relevant in practice.

(4) *Incidental implied authority.* Finally, agents are also given authority to do everything necessary, or ordinarily incidental, to the other actual authority conferred on them expressly or impliedly. This is probably best explained as an example of the business efficacy test in practice: it applies where, without such additional authority, an agent's mandate would be incoherent and unworkable.

SCEPTICISM ABOUT ACTUAL AUTHORITY

Agency sceptics deny that there is anything unique in express or implied actual authority, and that it can be rationalised by reference to the offer, acceptance and objective agreement ultimately reached between the principal and the third party. As Oliver Wendell Holmes Jnr explained (Holmes 1890–91, 348):

> So far as [the agent] expresses his principal's assent to be bound to the terms to be fixed by the agent, he is a mere messenger; in fixing the terms he is a stranger to the contract as if it had been made before his personal function began. The agent is simply a voice affording the marks provided by the principal's own expression of what he undertakes.

This analysis still has its advocates (for example, Krebs 2010) but the idea that the agent is essentially a messenger acting as the voice of the principal obviously underrepresents the independent discretionary power often wielded by agents and it does not fit with modern commercial practice where most principals are companies who can only act by agents and cannot otherwise express themselves.

Further obstacles to agency scepticism are that (i) actual authority can bind principal and third party even when the third party does not know, and could not reasonably have known, that the agent was actually an agent and (ii) actual authority can be conferred and operate retrospectively. These two phenomena are impossible to justify by reference to contract law and underlines that there is in fact something unique about the authority conferred by agreement between principal and agent. We consider these in turn next.

UNDISCLOSED ACTUAL AUTHORITY

Where the agent initially appears to be dealing on its own behalf, the hidden principal can sue and be sued on the contract after he 'intervenes' on the contract. Intervention has three pre-conditions.

First, the agent must have been acting at the time with actual authority, either express or implied. As we have seen, that requires looking at the objective agreement between principal and agent as to the latter's authority at the relevant time.

Second, when transacting with the third party, the agent must have intended to be exercising that actual authority. Until recently this was thought to be a question of subjective intention. However, in *Magellan Spirit ApS v Vitol SA* [2016] 1 CLC 480, Leggatt J said (at [16]–[20])

that the agent's *exercise* of actual authority should be assessed on an objective basis. But the Court's analysis in *Magellan* then focused on whether actual authority *existed*, which, as we have seen, is undoubtedly an objective question. The decision is best re-explained on that basis. Otherwise, this second requirement adds little to nothing to the first.

Third, the terms of the contract cannot exclude the possibility of intervention either expressly or impliedly. In other words, this is a form of default rule. While in principle this is a 'sticky' default rule, and the courts are loath to construe the contract to exclude the doctrine (*Siu Yin Kwan v Eastern Insurance Co Ltd (The Ospery)* [1994] 2 AC 199, 207 (per Lord Lloyd)), in practice the courts are very ready to do this. In *Kaefer Aislamientos SA de CV v AMS Drilling Mexico SA de CV* [2019] 1 WLR 3514, an entire agreement clause was held sufficient to exclude intervention. In *Bell v Ivy Technology Ltd* [2022] EWHC 1218 (Comm), a boilerplate clause excluding the Contracts (Rights of Third Parties) Act 1999 was held to exclude intervention.

It is sometimes said that there is also some form of 'bad faith' bar on intervention. The decision in *Said v Butt* [1920] 3 KB 497 (KB) is usually cited for the proposition that intervention may be banned if the third party had a particular reason for *not* dealing with the undisclosed principal, and *Collins v Associated Greyhound Racecourses Ltd* [1930] 1 Ch 1 is usually cited for cases where the third party had a particular reason *for* dealing with the undisclosed agent. Space precludes further discussion here, but there is an argument that in fact these cases actually turn on implied terms excluding intervention (Day 2022, 82–88).

Because undisclosed agency cannot be explained on the objective terms of the agreement between principal and third party, it has variously been described as anomalous and contrary to fundamental principles of contract law (see, for example, Pollock 1887, 359; Ames 1909, 443). That argument is exposed as fallacious once agency is treated as its own branch of the law, separate from contract. As Tan has put it (Tan 2004, 485): 'it makes no more sense to say that the undisclosed principal doctrine is anomalous when measured by contract principles than it is to say that the doctrine of privity of contract is anomalous because it is inconsistent with the undisclosed principal doctrine'. Nonetheless, the tension with contract law probably explains why the courts are in practice so willing to exclude the possibility of intervention at the third stage of the analysis.

JUSTIFYING UNDISCLOSED ACTUAL AUTHORITY

There have been various attempts to justify undisclosed agency. There are three principal schools of thought (for further detail see Day 2022, 68–77):

(1) *Commercial convenience.* It has been said that undisclosed agency exists because it is commercially useful to transact in this way. This is said to be 'beyond dispute' (Tan 2004, 481–85) but this is not convincing. Mercantile juries famously refused to recognise the rule, despite the best efforts of the judiciary: *Scrimshire v Alderton* (1743) 2 Strat 1182. That suggests there was no overwhelming demand in practice for this doctrine when it was developed. And there would probably be very little impact on modern commercial life if this doctrine was abolished. Where agents wish to protect their networks, they can act on a unnamed basis, making clear that they are acting for a principal without identifying them.

The doctrine appears to have been developed by judges in the eighteenth century (over mercantile objections) to avoid a perceived prejudice caused to the principal by the credit risk of the agent, and in particular the risk of insolvency (Fridman 2016, 72). It is not clear that such a doctrine is required for that purpose because the agent would hold any rights received under the contract on trust for the principal: Ames 1909, 448. Since the rights would be held on trust, they would not fall into the insolvent estate, so the doctrine was developed to guard against a risk that did not actually exist. This is actually a more orthodox approach to the question of insolvency risk, since (as we will explore in chapter six) the insolvency outcome is then simply conditioned by pre-existing proprietary entitlements rather than any special doctrine.

In any event, the commercial advantage of mitigating the insolvency risk of the intermediary has to be balanced against the fact that this doctrine (i) detracts from the certainty of counterparty otherwise provided by the objective principle in contract, and (ii) overrides parties' abilities to choose their counterparties contrary to freedom of contract.

(2) *Principal's contract theory.* In *Keighley, Maxsted & Co v Durant* [1901] AC 240, 261 Lord Lindley justified the doctrine on the basis that 'in truth, although not in form' the third party's contract all along was with the principal. Various scholars have adopted this theory. Müller-Freinfels, for example, argued that the principal should be treated as privy to

the contract because he 'ultimately bears the burden of the detriment, which is the consideration moving to the third party' and the agent is 'a mere conduit pipe' (Müller-Freinfels 1953, 306). Tan reached the same conclusion by a different route. Relying on Diplock LJ's 'assumption' in *Teheran-Europe Co Ltd v ST Belton (Tractors) Ltd* [1968] 2 QB 545, 555 that commercial parties should ordinarily be 'assumed' to be relaxed as to the identity of their counterparty, he argued that a third party impliedly agrees to contract with *both* the agent, and the agent's undisclosed principal, should there be one (Tan 2004, 501–05).

This is not persuasive. To begin with, the *Teheran-Europe* assumption is unsound. Commercial parties normally *do* care about who their counterparty is; indeed, the market exists precisely to enable parties to choose their counterparties. Further, as the third party has no knowledge that the agent was an agent at all, it is difficult to see how there could be any objective intention to by the third party to contract with the agent and any else the agent was secretly acting for. More recently, the argument has shifted to focus on a term implied in law (Tan 2021). This is said to be implied as a matter of policy for the commercial justifications considered above. But even if those commercial justifications were good ones, this theory still would not work: implication in law 'gap fills' within a contract after the contractual relationship between the parties has been identified and categorised (such as a contract for the sale of goods, insurance, employment).

(3) *Agent's contract theory.* The final set of theories recognise – correctly – that the contract is originally concluded between third party and agent but that the agent's rights and liabilities are extended to the principal. This has been described as 'primitive and highly restricted form of assignment' (Goodhart and Hamson 1932, 352), although that was doubted by the Privy Council in *Siu Yin Kwan*. The extension of rights and liabilities to the principal has to be justified by reference to relationship between agent and principal.

It has been said that the agent is committed to give the contract to the principal as a matter of fiduciary duty (Higgins 1965, 170–71) or by reference to consensual obligations between principal and agent (Barnett 1987, 1980–84). But the unspoken assumption in these explanations is that agency still has been justified by reference to other branches of the law.

There is much to commend a more straightforward approach that simply acknowledges that undisclosed agency represents a 'distinctive agency power', arising from the conferral of actual authority, and the rights which are created as between principal and third party are not contractual in nature: Seavey 1920, 877–78. It arises from a 'triple helix' of (i) the conferral of actual authority to enter into contracts on an undisclosed basis, (ii) the fiduciary duty of the agent to hold the benefit of that contract for the principal, and (iii) the ongoing rights of control which the principal has over the agent (Day 2022, 77).

Whatever the justification, the continued existence of the doctrine does at least make clear that actual authority is an independent phenomenon which cannot simply be explained away by reference to the contract between principal and third party. Agency sceptics such as Holmes and Krebs have no good answer to this.

RETROSPECTIVE ACTUAL AUTHORITY

Ratification also cannot simply be explained away by reference to orthodox principles of contract law. Ratification arises where the agent had no actual authority at the time of transacting but is given actual authority after the event. It is often described as a 'unilateral act of the will': *Harrison & Crossfield Ltd v London & North-Western Railway Co* [1917] 2 KB 755, 758 (per Rowlatt J). But it in fact arises from an agreement in the same way as actual authority conferred before the act. The act of the would-be-agent is an offer to act as such, which is then accepted by the act of ratification by the principal (Fridman 2017, 47–48).

The main reason why ratification cannot be absorbed into contract doctrine is because it has retrospective effect. The agent is treated as having had actual authority at the time of contracting, and the principal and third party are thus treated as having always been in a contract, even though they were not before the act of ratification. So, for example, in *Bolton Partners v Lambert* (1889) 41 Ch D 295, a third party offered to buy a lease of a factory from a principal. The offer was accepted by the agent without authority. The third party then tried to pull out of the deal because he was unhappy with the terms. Only then did the principal ratify its agent's act and sue the third party for breach of contract. The principal was successful, despite the fact that the offer had been withdrawn before its authorised acceptance, precisely because of the retrospective nature of this doctrine.

The threefold test for ratification is similar in structure to the test for allowing interventions by undisclosed principals.

First, the acts of offer and acceptance that trigger retrospective authority are assessed objectively. For the offer, that means that the agent must have claimed, when so acting, to have been acting as agent. The unauthorised acts of undisclosed agents cannot therefore be retrospectively authorised because, objectively, at the time they were acting for themselves: *Keighley, Maxsted & Co v Durant* [1901] AC 240. As for acceptance, as in contract law, this can be express or implied. Normally there must at least be some positive act but, in theory, silence and inaction might, objectively, be taken as acceptance of the relevant act made by the agent.

Second, when accepting the offer of agency, the principal must also have had, or ought to have had, knowledge of the material facts concerning the would-be-agent's acts. While this requirement is normally expressed in terms of knowledge, it makes more sense to think of this as being about intention: the principal must be intending to confer actual authority on the agent. This is the mirror image of the second stage of the test for intervention in cases of undisclosed agency where, on an orthodox analysis, the principal has to show that the agent actually intended to exercise actual authority (see pages 59–60 above).

Third, because of its retrospective effect, ratification is a potentially very powerful tool in the hands of a principal. It is therefore subject to various limitations in the same way as intervention by an undisclosed principal on an agent's contract. So, for example, ratification cannot be used to retrospectively meet a deadline which has been missed under the contract or set by law (such as limitation). More than that, ratification must be made within a reasonable period of time: if principals wait too long, the law will make the election for them. Ratification also cannot be used to interfere with vested property rights. Nor can ratification be used by corporate principals to do an act which they could not have done themselves at the time. And a principal cannot cherry-pick when ratifying an act: the contract must be authorised as a whole or not at all. These limitations might be grouped together under a principle against ratification causing 'unfair prejudice' to the third party: *Smith v Henniker-Major & Co* [2003] Ch 182, at [71] (per Robert Walker LJ). This looks similar to a 'bad faith' bar to intervention in undisclosed agency, if it exists (see page 60 above).

The fact that the agreement between a principal and agent conferring actual authority on an agent can work not only prospectively but also, if the parties so chose, retrospectively – so long as unfair prejudice is not caused to others – is another example of conceptual distinctiveness of agency. Agency sceptics say that it is simply anomalous and wrong and should be abolished (Krebs 2010, 214–18). However, it is capable of rational justification. As between principal and agent, the outcome is justified by the agency agreement constituted by the act of ratification. As for the third party, the critical point is that the agent must always have been working on a *disclosed* basis. The third party cannot complain to having been bound from the beginning given they originally entered into the contract on the objective basis that the agent was working for the principal.

THE APPEARANCE OF ACTUAL AUTHORITY

So far we have considered variants of actual authority, where it can fairly be said that the agent truly has a mandate from the principal, either at the time of acting or retrospectively. The same cannot be said when only the doctrine of 'apparent' or 'ostensible' authority is engaged. As the label suggests, in this scenario there is the objective appearance of actual authority. The question which then arises is: should the *appearance* of actual authority be treated as having the same transactional effect as the *existence* of actual authority?

The dominant systems for global commerce – English law and US law – provide different responses to that question. US law answers 'yes'. This can be justified by the general principle of objectivity in contract law. The same approach could in principle be taken in English law. Identifying the parties to a contract is a question of construction: see, for example, *Homburg Houtimport BV v Agrosin Private Ltd (The Starsin)* [2004] 1 AC 715. The test is whether a reasonable person, having regard to the factual matrix, would understand that the third party and principal have respectively offered to be, and have accepted being, party to the contract. When the factual matrix includes a shared understanding that one party is acting on behalf of a principal, the reasonable person should conclude that the contract is between the agent and third party, even if in reality (and despite objective appearances) the agent has no actual authority to enter into the relevant transaction (see, for example, Conant 1968, 683–86). In disclosed agency cases, it is usually obvious when one person appears to be acting for another because of the circumstances, such as how they introduce themselves, choose their modes of communication, present themselves in correspondence and sign off any documentation.

These are the circumstances which the reasonable person would take into account when identifying the parties.

However, at present, the orthodox position in English law is that apparent authority 'operates as an estoppel, preventing the principal from asserting that he is not bound by the contract': *Freeman & Lockyer (A Firm) v Buckhurst Park Properties (Mangal) Ltd* [1964] 2 QB 480, 503 (per Diplock LJ). In other words, apparent authority is a defence which a third party can raise when the principal wishes to argue that the agent lacked actual authority. But it cannot be used by the principal to sue the third party on the contract; the principal must ratify the contract (see pages 63–65 above) before suing on it.

This asymmetry of outcome on the estoppel approach makes no sense and is unnecessarily complicated. It is difficult to see what ratification adds in this context: there are no conceivable circumstances in which a principal could be fairly barred from ratifying a contract on which it could nonetheless be sued by the third party.

Another aspect of apparent authority is potentially not so readily explained by the objective principle. There is no apparent authority where the third party knew or ought to have known that the agent lacked actual authority. In *Thanakharn Kasikorn Thai Chamkat (Mahachon) v Akai Holdings Ltd (in liquidation)* (2010) 13 HKCFAR 479, Lord Neuberger NPJ modified this reliance test: he held that the principal is not bound after having held out an intermediary as having authority in a transaction where the third party acts dishonestly or irrationally when dealing with the unauthorised agent, including where the third party subjectively turns a blind eye or is reckless to the lack of actual authority.

The decision has been criticised for moving away from an objective test and also on the basis that the process of determining whether apparent authority is made out is ultimately a single process, rather than a rigid two-step process of finding a holding out, and then inquiring as to the third party's state of knowledge (see Watts 2015, 48–56). That criticism was accepted by Lord Kitchin in *East Asia Company Ltd v PT Satria Tirtatama Energindo (Bermuda)* [2019] UKPC 30, who largely restored the orthodox (and objective) approach to question of when a third party is on inquiry as to a lack of actual authority. The question of whether there has been a representation of authority, and reliance on it, is now to be tested from the perspective of the reasonable person with all background knowledge reasonably available to the parties. In other words, the assessment is made using the same factual matrix as would be available if the contract were simply being construed.

Apparent authority also ill-fits the usual test for estoppel. Despite this, ever since *Rama Corp LD v Proved Tin and General Investment LD* [1952] 2 QB 147, it has become trite in English law to ask whether (i) the principal has made or permitted a representation of actual authority, (ii) the third party has relied on that representation and (iii) the third party has as a result changed their position. However, whereas for orthodox estoppels the representation has to be clear and unambiguous, for apparent estoppel the representation can be very general and vague, and it is readily implied from the circumstances in which the principal permits the agent to operate. Further, the other requirements – that there be a change of position in reliance on that representation – add little if anything to the analysis. It appears to suffice that the third party has entered into the contract, which, of course, it must have done in the first place in order to be attempting to enforce it against the principal. Given these points of difference from typical estoppels, this must at best a special (and weak) type of estoppel – in other words, not really an estoppel at all.

Despite this, English law shows no sign of abandoning the estoppel analysis. This is probably because of some inherent discomfort in the idea of binding the principal to a contract to which they otherwise never consented. The notion of a representation emanating from, or at least permitted by, the principal provides a justification for that outcome. In those circumstances, it can be said the principal caused the third party to enter into the contract and so should be held responsible for consequences.

However, once due weight is given to objectivity in contract law, this concern about the principal's lack of consent to the contract should fall away. Agreement in contract law is assessed objectively not subjectively. In all apparent authority cases, there is an objective agreement between third party and principal because a reasonable person would understand the agent to acting with actual authority on behalf of the principal. Apparent authority is therefore best regarded as simply a function of the relationship between the objective principle and actual authority. To that extent at least, agency sceptics like Krebs are right (their error instead lies in the wider claim of the rest of agency law lacks conceptual distinctiveness).

COMMUNICATING AGENTS

One unfortunate consequence of the estoppel approach is that English law has tied itself in contradictions about whether, and when, agents themselves can provide the representations that create their apparent authority. In *Armagas Ltd v Mundogas SA (The Ocean Frost)* [1986] AC 717, the third party knew that the agent lacked authority to sign a charterparty. However, the agent pretended to the third party that he had telephoned senior management to obtain authority as a one-off. Both the Court of Appeal and the House of Lords questioned whether agents were ever entitled to self-authorise themselves in this way, casting doubt on the submission that 'ostensible authority of an agent to communicate agreement by his principal to a particular transaction is conceptually different from ostensible authority to enter into that particular transaction': at 779 (per Lord Keith, approving 731 (per Robert Goff LJ)).

However, in *First Energy (UK) Ltd v Hungarian International Bank Ltd* [1993] 2 Lloyd's Rep 194, the Court of Appeal reached the opposite conclusion on similar facts. There, a bank customer knew that the bank manager with whom it was dealing lacked actual authority to offer credit lines but then received a letter from the bank manager doing just that. The Court of Appeal held that the bank manager did have apparent authority to make a representation of fact as to the decision reached within the bank, and the letter had been sent within the scope of that apparent authority. The distinction with *Armagas* might be that, in *First Energy*, the agent himself had informed the third party of the limitation on his actual authority, and so he was changing his own previous representation rather than that of his principal.

Matters were made a little clearer by *Kelly v Fraser* [2013] 1 AC 450. There, the third party sought a transfer of his pension entitlements. Only the trustees of the pension scheme could approve a transfer, as the third party well knew, but he was wrongly told by a colleague in the human resources department at work (to whom the trustees had delegated administrative functions) that the transfer had taken place. Lord Sumption held that the trustees were bound by the communication of their unauthorised agent, and in so doing, purportedly affirmed both *Armagas* and *First Energy*. There is a suggestion in the case that *Armagas* should be confined to its 'complex and extraordinary facts' (at [12]) although *Armagas* was also said to contain 'the classic statement of the relevant legal principles' (at [15]). Overall, however, the general gist of Lord Sumption's reasoning is contrary to the spirit of *Armagas*, because he held that it was also 'perfectly possible' for a principal to hold out subordinates as (ibid):

> the persons who are to communicate to outsiders the fact that it has been approved by those who are authorised to approve it or that some particular agent has been duly authorised to approve it. These are representations which, if made by someone held out by the company to make representations of that kind, may give rise to an estoppel.

The development of the 'communicating agent' sits uncomfortably with the general rule in English law that a principal should only be held to an agent's contract if it made or permitted a representation to be made that the agent had authority to conclude the contract. The communicating agent can bind a principal to a contract even where no such representation as to authority has been made, through the agent making a representation as to the conclusion of an agreement. These conceptual difficulties could be avoided by adopting the objective consent approach to apparent authority.

AUTHORITY BY ESTOPPEL

Estoppel may be relevant beyond the context of apparent authority. To begin with, an estoppel may arise where, after the transaction, the principal represents, or has encouraged the impression, that the unauthorised was authorised. That would prevent the principal not from denying the existence of the contract but rather from denying the existence of authority. However, this is a normal type of estoppel and the representation must be clear and unequivocal. It only applies in circumstances where the principal either makes an express representation of the agent's authority after the event (which may, in any event, constitute ratification) or, knowing both (i) of the unauthorised act and (ii) the mistaken reliance placed on it by the third party as an authorised act, the principal continues to deal with the third party in such a way that could only be taken to be consistent with the agent's act having been authorised: *Spiro v Lintern* [1973] 1 WLR 1002.

There might also be a role for true estoppel (that is, not the weak and special estoppel arising from apparent authority) in cases like *First*

Energy and *Kelly v Fraser* where a principal decides only to communicate with third parties using communicating agents and the third party has no other way of learning when a transaction has been concluded (see Watts 2020, 261–62).

It has also been argued that an authority may arise from estoppel where an agent is put in charge of the principal's business and allowed to run it in the agent's own name, the representation being that the agent and principal are one and the same person (Tettenborn 1998). This suggestion was made to explain *Watteau v Fenwick* [1893] 1 QB 346, a case which is otherwise impossible to justify on any orthodox basis.

In *Watteau v Fenwick*, the agent managed Victoria Hotel in Stockton for the principal but on an undisclosed basis. The principal forbade the agent from buying anything other than bottled ales and mineral water from third party suppliers; the principal would supply the rest. In breach of this limitation on his actual authority, the agent bought cigars and bovril from the claimant on credit. Wills J held that 'the principal is liable for all the acts of the agent which are within the authority usually confided to an agent of that character' (at 348). The claimant was therefore allowed to sue the undisclosed principal for the sums due, despite the agent not acting with actual authority (given the principal's instructions) or apparent authority (given the undisclosed nature of the agency), and there being no freestanding doctrine of 'usual authority' in English law.

Tettenborn's re-interpretation of *Watteau v Fenwick* neatly sidesteps the problems with a previous attempt to justify the decision turning on apparent ownership (Conant 1968, 687–88), which would involve extending that doctrine in an unprincipled way from dealings in property (apparent ownership is discussed further at pages 78–81 below). However, Tettenborn's own approach has potentially wide-ranging consequences. The estoppel would apply to many undisclosed agency relationships, rendering the principal liable on a contract even if intervention were not possible (but contrast pages 59–60 above).

Another unsatisfactory re-explanation – which cleanly excises *Watteau v Fenwick* from the law of agency altogether – would be to treat it as a claim in unjust enrichment, since the undisclosed principal benefited from the supply of the goods on credit without otherwise being contractually liable to pay for them (Tan 2017, 62). The problem with this explanation is that it is difficult to see what ground for restitution applies to the claim in *Watteau v Fenwick* itself.

In the US, *Watteau v Fenwick* limps on. *Restatement Third, Agency* states that the undisclosed principal ought to be liable notwithstanding any internal limitations on an agent's actual authority in the same way as in disclosed agency cases. This is justified on the basis that it protects the reasonable expectations of third parties, and avoids 'opportunistic' speculation by the principal (American Law Institute 2006, §2.06). This is unconvincing because the third party by definition had no reasonable expectation to be able to sue anyone other than the undisclosed agent. In contrast, outside of the US, *Watteau v Fenwick* appears to have no future: it has been doubted in England (*Rhodian River Shipping Co SA and Rhodian Sailor Shipping Co SA v Halla Maritime Corp* [1984] 1 Lloyd's Rep 373, 378–79 (per Bingham J)) and Australia (*International Paper Co v Spicer* (1906) 4 CLR 739, 763 (per Isaacs J)) and overturned in Canada (*Sign-O-Lite Plastics Ltd v Metropolitan Life Insurance Co* (1990) 73 DLR (4th) 541, 548 (per Wood JA)).

AUTHORITY IMPOSED BY LAW

Agents are sometimes authorised by statute rather than agreement. This normally arises outside the commercial context, such as under s 5 of the Mental Capacity Act 2005. It can also be said that the initial corporate authority conferred by the primary rules of attribution are imposed by law rather than by agreement, because it emanates from the company's constitution (Leow 2019, 105). However, the company constitution is a form of agreement between the company and its members: Companies Act 2006, s 33. The better view is that this initial authority is still the product of consent, and so can fairly be treated as a form of actual authority. In contrast, when a company becomes insolvent, officeholders such as liquidators and administrators are clearly statutory agents (see chapter six) whose authority is imposed on the company and its stakeholders by law.

It is sometimes said that the common law also imposes authority by operation of law in 'agency of necessity' cases. This is wrong. These are cases where someone has undertaken a reasonable course of action with the intention of preventing harm to another's property or person and it appeared at the time that, but for such a course of action, harm would befall the property or person in question. The two questions which arise are (i) whether the person or owner is bound by the acts of the intervener and (ii) if so, whether the former should be remunerated by the latter. The historic cases involve shipmasters and acceptors for honour of bills of exchange. As to cases raising the former question, these could today probably be decided the same way by using the more liberal approaches to implied actual authority and apparent authority that have subsequently developed. As to the latter issue, the right to remuneration is best regarded as a correlative right arising alongside that consensual authority. Attempts to reconceptualise this remuneration right as a claim in unjust enrichment is deeply problematic, but it is not necessary to discuss this further here (see Day 2016).

4

Title

Dealings with assets such as goods and debts raise further proprietary issues which are considered in this chapter. The focus is on the question of title disputes. A title dispute arises when two parties claim to have the better right to property, and therefore the better right to control and benefit from it to the exclusion of the other. This could arise in a number of scenarios. For example, the original owner could purport to sell to two parties, A and B, one after the other. Or the seller may not be the owner at all but sells to B; the earlier owner, A, then makes himself known. Who has the better claim out of A and B? This is often asked in terms of who should be given 'priority'. In practice, the questions are pressing not only when the property is unique and so its loss cannot properly be compensated through the payment of damages; they also matter when the seller poses a credit risk and so may not pay any damages which arise from failure to transfer title.

1. THE TWO PRINCIPLES

In title disputes arising out of commercial transactions, there are two principles which operate in tension with each other. These are the property principle and the transaction principle: *Bishopsgate Motor Finance Corp v Transport Brakes Ltd* [1949] AC 322, 336–37 (per Denning LJ).

THE PROPERTY PRINCIPLE

The essence of a property right is the control it confers over the asset in question (see page 5 above). Ownership is the best possible property right and, as a starting point, permits the owner to exclude the world from the asset. Control conferred by an ownership right over an asset therefore results in various incidents, such as entitlement to use of and income and capital from the property, most famously explored in Honoré 1961. However, this is only a starting point. An ownership right is subject to any limited property rights, such as those conferred by security and bailment, which can subordinate various incidents of ownership during their existence. In this sense, ownership can be characterised as having a residual character, or a 'bundle' of rights from which there can be derogation.

If we take this concept of ownership over property seriously, it also tells us what the priority rule should be. When two parties claim to be owners to the same property, the person whose interest was created or conferred earlier (A) ought to have priority. The right to control conferred on A at that earlier point in time includes the right to determine when to transfer that right of control to another. It would be contrary to that right to allow a subsequent person (B) to assert a better claim of ownership. This is sometimes called the 'first in time rule' – A being first in time to B – but typically is still described by the Latin phrase *nemo dat quod non habet*, or *nemo plus iuris transferre ad alium potest ipse habet*, or just plain old '*nemo dat*' for convenience. Adapted into English, it means this: only the owner can transfer or confer that right of ownership onto another.

THE TRANSACTION PRINCIPLE

The criticism made of the property principle is that a purchaser who has acted in good faith and without notice of the prior owner's interest will suffer, despite lacking fault. It may be thought better to give effect to the transaction purporting to confer title to property rather than to the underlying property right. Adopting a transaction principle which protects innocent buyers removes that perceived injustice and provides certainty to all purchasers entering into such transactions, for the benefit of commercial dealings more generally. Further, where an owner voluntarily parts with possession of property, the owner is taking a risk and should not 'put the consequences of his own mistaken judgment on to the shoulders of a blameless third party' (Goode and McKendrick 2020, 495).

The transaction principle has powerful and persuasive advocates, with many calls for an 'entrusting rule', invoking the language of (but not quite the same rule as) the US Uniform Commercial Code (in addition to Goode and McKendrick 2020, see Tettenborn 2018). However, the case for its adoption is ultimately unconvincing for two reasons.

First, if the transaction principle is allowed to make inroads into the property principle, the greater certainty given to transactions needs to be balanced against an increased uncertainty as to the security of property rights acquired *by* that transaction. An innocent buyer would be more likely to find that they could lose their property in due course to another innocent buyer. While commercial parties want to transact with confidence to acquire new assets, they equally want to be confident that the property they already own or buy cannot be taken away from them without their consent by others. When presented with this trade-off between the transaction principle and the property principle, it is not clear that commercial interests necessarily demand favouring the former over the latter.

Second, it is wrong to assume that commercial purchasers inevitably lose out from a strict application of the property principle. Contract law provides other remedies. In particular, the purchaser's interest in obtaining title to the property will normally be driven by economic considerations, which can be adequately redressed by a pecuniary remedy paid by the seller. As discussed in chapter five, the purchaser can enforce a claim in damages for loss caused by the breach of contract. That would indemnify the purchaser for any liability in the tort of conversion. The purchaser can also sue in unjust enrichment to recover the purchase price. It is thus only where the seller is a credit risk that there will be a permanent loss to a commercial purchaser. As will be explored further in chapter six, there are ways of structuring transactions to mitigate against that particular risk. Where those mitigating steps have not been taken, it is not obvious that the loss should still be reallocated to the original owner by depriving him of his otherwise superior title.

DIFFERENT STARTING POINTS IN COMMON AND CIVIL LAW

Despite the difficulties with its underlying justification, modern civil law systems largely endorse the transaction principle. For example, the German *Bürgerliches Gesetzbuch*, or Civil Code, provides that anyone receiving goods in good faith from a person they believe to be the owner or agent of the owner acquires ownership in priority to the previous true owner unless either (i) the property was stolen from the owner, went missing or was lost in some other way or (ii) the purchaser was grossly negligent in not realising the seller was not the true owner. French law is guided by a similar, but slightly narrower, notion of '*en fair en meubles, law possession vaut titre*', which essentially means that good faith receipt of possession by a purchaser confers superior title on the purchaser.

In contrast, the common law – quite rightly, it is suggested, for the reasons already given – adopted the property principle as the starting point. References to the principle of *nemo dat* in the case law can be traced back at least as far as the seventeenth century, and probably earlier. Sir Mackenzie Chalmers hardwired it into the Sale of Goods Act, crediting it as having intellectual foundations going back to Roman law (Chalmers 1890, 39). Section 21 of the Sale of Goods Act 1979 now states, as a general rule, that 'where goods are sold by a person who is not their owner ... the buyer acquires no better title to the goods than the seller'. A similar principle exists for other forms of property. However, the courts and Parliament have also developed numerous exceptions to that general rule of *nemo dat* in English law. Advocates of the transaction principle suggest that the existence of these exceptions show there is something wrong with that general rule. However, as we will see shortly, the common law 'exceptions' are in fact not exceptions at all. And while the statutory interventions are departures from the general rule, they are open to criticism on their own terms, as we will also see in this chapter.

One criticism of the current law is worth addressing up front. This is that the present departures in English law from *nemo dat* are piecemeal, incoherent and produce an 'arbitrary and unpredictable mess' (Tettenborn 2018, 177). That is undoubtedly true: no one seriously attempts to defend the status quo in English law, which is profoundly unsatisfactory. The US Uniform Commercial Code, which moved US law away from its English law origins, is often held up as an exemplar of the type of simpler statutory reform to which the UK should aspire. The primary argument advanced in this chapter is that the law would be in a better state if English law showed greater fidelity to the property principle. However, if English law is to make a decisive move towards the transactional principle, then the American approach is undoubtedly preferable for its simplicity and, consequently, its greater predictability in operation.

2. COMMON LAW 'EXCEPTIONS' TO THE PROPERTY PRINCIPLE

Chalmers codified four common law 'exceptions' when drafting the Sale of Goods Act, one of which ('market overt') has since been abolished. Although the market overt exception had been a clear adoption of the transaction principle, none of the remaining three exceptions represent a true departure from the property principle. That is because the effect for each remaining exception is not that the buyer takes the property free of any defects at all but rather than it takes free of the particular defects in the seller's title, as conferred on it.

VOIDABLE TITLE

Section 23 of the Sale of Goods Act 1979 provides:

> When the seller of goods has a voidable title to them, but his title has not been avoided at the time of the sale, the buyer acquires a good title to the goods, provided he buys them in good faith and without notice of the seller's defect of title.

This rule is not an exception to *nemo dat*. Rather, it is a product of the type of prior property right which exists in this scenario. Imagine A sells goods to B induced by a misrepresentation and B sells the goods to C before A purports to rescind the contract with B. Prior to rescinding the contract, A cannot be described as the 'owner'; the only property right which A has in the goods is a 'mere equity'. As a weak form of equitable interest, a mere equity has a lower priority than a subsequent legal interest acquired by the good faith purchaser for value without notice. Section 23 merely embodies the rule about the limited nature of a mere equity in property.

AGENCY

Section 21 of the Sale of Goods Act 1979 itself recognises that a non-owner seller can validly transfer title on having 'authority or consent' from the owner to sell. This is also not an exception to *nemo dat*. It is simply an application of the agency principles we discussed in chapter three. If the seller acts with the actual or apparent authority of the title-holder, they can transfer title to the goods, much in the same way as an agent can contract on behalf of principle. Apparent authority, in particular, is a useful tool for striking some balance between the property principle and the transaction principle.

ESTOPPEL

Section 21 also recognises that the owner can 'by his conduct' be 'precluded from denying the seller's authority to sell'. This is not the same as apparent authority, discussed at pages 65–67 above, which acts to preclude the owner from denying being in a contract with the buyer. But nor is this a true departure from *nemo dat*; it is simply an application of estoppel in the sales context. As the great early modern jurist, Sir Edward Coke, explained, the effect of an estoppel is to: 'stoppeth or closeth up [a person's mouth] to allege or plead the truth' (Coke 1628, 252a). In the context of a title dispute, this means that the owner is prevented from setting up their earlier ownership interest as the basis for claiming the property.

An orthodox estoppel requires, in general terms, (i) a clear and unambiguous representation, (ii) reliance by the recipient of that representation, leading to (iii) some change of position by the recipient. The relevant representation is that the seller is the owner, hence the label 'apparent ownership' sometimes given to this doctrine. It would be unusual for an owner to say that in terms, and the focus in the case law is instead on whether the owner impliedly made such a representation.

The starting point is that, if an owner puts a third party in possession of goods (or in a position where they can give instructions as to their possession), that does not constitute a clear and unambiguous representation that that person is themselves the owner. That is obviously right: possession and ownership are not the same thing. Instead, the owner must have done something more. But quite what the 'something more' must be remains unclear, thanks in part to two difficult judgments of Lord Halsbury.

Henderson & Co v Williams [1895] 1 QB 521 is a rare case where an estoppel argument succeeded. The owner of 150 bags of sugar stored at the defendant's warehouse was tricked into instructing the defendant to hold the sugar 'to the order of' a fraudster (that is, attorn: see page 23 above), who then promptly sold it to the claimant, an innocent purchaser. The claimant contracted with the fraudster based on written assurances from the defendant that it held the sugar to the order of the fraudster and would do so thereafter to the claimant's order. When the fraud came to light, the owner instructed the warehouse to withhold the sugar from the purchasers. Lord Halsbury held that the sugar should be released. The owner was precluded from so instructing the warehouse, because it had 'given the indicia of title to another so as to enable him to pass as the true owner' (at 527).

Lord Halsbury was forced to clarify his approach in *Farquharson Bros & Co v King & Co* [1902] AC 325. There, the fraudster was the owner's own clerk, Mr Capon, who had abused his position to sell his employer's timber to himself as a broker under the false name 'Mr Brown', and then as 'Mr Brown' onto innocent purchasers. The owners had not made any representation that Mr Capon had a 'disposing power', and indeed the purchasers had understood themselves to be dealing with the false persona 'Mr Brown', not Mr Capon and so cannot have been acting on any representation from the owners as to Mr Capon's position. The fact that the owners had 'enabled' Mr Capon's fraud by employing him as their clerk in the first place, and then not monitoring his actions, was neither here nor there. But Lord Halsbury then added confusion by saying (at 332):

> it depends on the sense in which you are to understand the word 'enabled' …
> in one sense every man who sells a pistol or a dagger enables an intending murderer to commit a crime; but is he, in selling a pistol or a dagger to some person who comes to buy in his shop, acting in breach of any duty?

In the modern law, the rules on the 'something more than mere possession' question now appears to have settled around two propositions.

First, the owner can confer some document on the seller that enables the seller to hold itself out as being in possession *as owner*, and so confers 'indicia of title' as Lord Halsbury put it in *Henderson* itself. Railway receipts for groundnuts were not good enough in *Mercantile Bank of India v Central Bank of India* [1938] AC 287 because it 'no more conveyed a representation that the merchants were entitled to dispose of the property than the actual possession of the goods themselves would have conveyed any such representation. It is not like a negotiable instrument' (per Lord Wright, at 303). Nor was the vehicle registration document for a car in *Central Newbury Car Auctions Ltd v Unity Finance* [1957] 1 QB 371, because it was a tax document which actually stated 'Important. The person in whose name a vehicle is registered may or may not be the legal owner of the vehicle'. In contrast, in *Eastern Distributors v Goldring* [1957] 2 QB 600, 611 (per Devlin J), the owner 'armed' the seller with signed blank hire purchase documents for his car that enabled the seller to 'represent that he was the owner'. This form of apparent ownership thus appears to have sensible and workable limits, and strikes an appropriate balance between the property principle and the transaction principle.

Second, building on Lord Halsbury's reference to 'breach of duty' in *Farquharson*, the courts have suggested that estoppel arises where the owner owes a duty of care to the buyer. This is a much less welcome development than the first form of apparent ownership. First of all, it wrongly conflates two entirely distinct doctrines, estoppel and negligence. The former, as Coke said, is about stopping someone asserting their prior ownership right otherwise open to them (but contrast Devlin J in *Eastern Distributors* at 611). The latter is about compensating a defendant for loss caused by breach of a duty of care. If a tortious duty of care arose between owner and buyer, the remedy would not be to preclude the owner from asserting rights of ownership but rather for the owner to pay damages to the buyer for the loss arising from that assertion of rights. A further objection to this doctrine is that it effectively amounts to 'estoppel by omission'; the issue here is not whether a representation has been made that the seller was the owner but whether representation should have been made that the seller was *not* the owner. But omissions duties are rarely imposed on any party unless assumed by contract, especially in the commercial context.

In any event, it would take very unusual facts in a sales context for such a duty of care in tort to arise, not least as the claim would be for pure economic loss. In *Mercantile Credit Co Ltd v Hamblin* [1962] 2 QB 242, an apparently respectable car dealer was asked by a consumer for advice about borrowing on the security of her car. At the dealer's request, she provided him with signed blank hire purchase forms. The dealer then purported to sell the car as his own to a finance company and conclude a hire purchase agreement for that car back to the consumer. At 275, Pearson LJ held that she owed a duty of care because she

was arming the dealer with the means to make a contract ostensibly on her behalf. In my judgment, there was a sufficient relationship of proximity between the defendant and any persons who might contract to provide her with the money that she was seeking, to impose upon her a duty of care with regard to the preparation and custody of the contractual documents. The duty was owing to those persons, whoever they might eventually be found to be. They were in fact the finance company.

It is doubtful *Hamblin* would be decided the same way today and is better regarded as a product of its time, when the tort of negligence was in expansionary mode. In *Hamblin*, it may have been reasonably foreseeable to the car owner that the dealer would show the forms to third parties in the context of seeking to raise finance; it was never reasonably foreseeable to the owner that the dealer would pretend that the car was his own and would sell it on that basis. A more robust approach was adopted by the House of Lords in *Moorgate Mercantile Co v Twitchings* [1977] AC 890, albeit with two Law Lords dissenting, where it was held that the owner owed no duty of care where they had failed to participate in a voluntary scheme to register a hire purchase agreement for the car. It was rightly pointed out it would be paradoxical for voluntary scheme could be used to impose a mandatory omissions duty in tort.

Even if a duty of care can be established, a claim in estoppel by negligence should still not normally succeed. That is because, after having found such a duty in *Hamblin*, at 275, Pearson LJ accepted (i) the duty would not be breached where (as on the facts of that case) it was reasonable for the owner to trust the seller with possession of the goods or documents that might enable them to purport to deal with the goods and (ii) the 'proximate or real cause was the fraud of the dealer' rather than any breach of duty by the owner. While the first point may not be available to the true owner in every *nemo dat* dispute, the second point is likely to be available on the facts of very many cases: most cases where estoppel by negligence is alleged will fail on causation grounds.

3. EXCEPTIONS CREATED BY THE FACTORS ACTS 1823–89

The three principal statutory exceptions to *nemo dat* in the sale of goods context are found in the Factors Act 1889. Space precludes discussion of specialised statutory priority rules such as for merchant shipping, company charges, financial collateral arrangements and under the Cape Town Convention, and in any event those exceptions are much less controversial.

HISTORICAL CONTEXT

To properly understand the Factors Acts exceptions, and why they are entirely unhelpful and unnecessary, it is necessary first to place them in their historical context. They were developed in the nineteenth century to facilitate the activities of factors.

Factors are not a feature of modern commercial life but, in the nineteenth century, they were at the heart of the economy. Factors were agents, often engaged in foreign trade, who acted on behalf of merchants to deal in commodities in return for receiving commission on the transactions (so-called factor*age*, not to be confused with factor*ing*: see page 42 above). Factors typically had possession of the commodities in question and operated on an unnamed or undisclosed agency basis. Third parties knew (at most) that the factor was acting in a ministerial capacity, but normally not for whom. The economic significance of factors by the eighteenth century lay in the fact that they also provided financial lubrication for international trade: they would regularly make advances to their principals, provide credit to third parties, and even assume some of the performance risk of the underlying transactions (Munday 1977).

The problem was that the common law struggled to give effect to the factor's role as financier. In particular, the very short law report of Lee CJ in *Paterson v Tash* (1743) 2 Str 1178 stated that 'though a factor has power to sell, and thereby bind his principal, yet he cannot bind or affect the property of the goods by pledging them as a security for his own debt'. The law report may not have been accurate (see Thomas 2011, 167–70) but that is by-the-by because at the time the courts faithfully adhered to the law report of that decision, even if they doubted its commercial efficacy. This caused a problem for factors because, while principals increasingly turned to them for credit advances, they were unable to raise capital themselves from external sources by offering as security their main body of assets, that is their principals' consignments.

In May 1823, the House of Commons was petitioned by the commercial communities in London, Liverpool and Bristol to change the law to allow factors to lend and borrow on the basis of the commodities or equivalent documents (such as bills of lading) in their possession. The arguments raised by them would seem familiar in any modern law reform debate: the market needed factors to be given access to this capital given their central role in financing commercial trade; the commercial practice was well-established, even though unsupported by the common law; and the common law was out of step with international standards, because factors in Scotland and continental Europe were permitted in law to give security over their principals' assets.

Following the petitions, a select committee was set up together comprising MPs and one non-Parliamentarian, the well-known commercial solicitor, James Freshfield (whose firm continues to this day to be amongst the leading firms in the City of London). They reported in June 1823 and recommended factors should be able to pledge their principals' goods in order to obtain credit, not least because growing commercial awareness that the supposed rule in *Paterson v Tash* was beginning to stifle capital sources for factors, and thereby threatened Britain's position at the centre of global trade. The report led to the Factors Act 1823, an exceptionally badly worded piece of legislation which – in light of opposition to the proposed reform led by Sir James Scarlett MP, later the judge known as Lord Abinger – did not go nearly as far as had been recommended.

The 1823 statutory exception to *nemo dat* was gradually widened by further Factors Acts in 1825, 1842 and 1877, before being put into its present form by a consolidating act in 1889. The Factors Act 1889 contains three exceptions to *nemo dat* for 'mercantile agents' (s 2), 'sellers in possession' (s 8) and 'buyers in possession' (s 9). Section 2 can be traced back to the 1825 Act. Sections 8 and 9 can be traced back to the 1877 Act, and responded to a narrow construction placed on the original mercantile agent restriction by the courts. As the great commercial judge, Scrutton LJ once acerbically remarked, while Parliament had not intended to apply 'artificial distinctions' to the mercantile agent exception, the 'history of the Factors Acts is restriction of their language by the Courts in favour of the true owner, followed by reversal of the Courts' decisions by the Legislature': *Folkes v King* [1923] 1 KB 282, 306.

Sections 8 and 9 are duplicated with immaterial differences in ss 24 and 25 of the Sale of Goods Act 1979; s 2 was not included in the codification, although there was no obviously good reason for Chalmers to omit it.

Three points can be made in light of this context to the Factors Acts. *First*, the pressure for this reform was not directly concerned with trade itself but instead was about facilitating the availability of credit to finance trade, which meant facilitating the ability of those lending to factors to mitigate credit risk by the taking of security.

Second, the pressure for reform largely took place before the modern law of apparent authority and apparent ownership had been solidified; it is doubtful that the Factors Acts would have been necessary (beyond the narrow question of overruling *Paterson v Tash*) if those doctrines had developed sooner.

Third, the commercial pressure which led to the creation of these *nemo dat* exceptions has now entirely gone. Factors were an important engine of the nineteenth century economy but are no longer a feature of the modern economy. Yet the statute books still feature these exceptions. The limited case law on them, much of it now relatively old, suggests they do not come up much in commercial practice.

CURRENT STATUTORY EXCEPTIONS

The three current Factors Act exceptions each adopt a similar structure and, simplifying somewhat, can be split into the same three constituent parts as set out below.

	(1) Seller	(2) Transaction	(3) Buyer
Mercantile Agent (s 2)	(a) Mercantile agent (b) In possession of goods or documents of title (c) With consent of owner	(a) Sale, pledge, or other disposition (b) Ordinary course of business	Good faith and without notice
Seller in Possession (s 8)	(a) Seller having already sold the goods (b) In possession of those goods or documents of title	(a) Sale, pledge, or other disposition (or agreement as to the same) (b) Delivery or transfer	Good faith and without notice
Buyer in Possession (s 9)	(a) Buyer (b) In possession of those goods or documents of title (c) With consent of owner	(a) Sale, pledge, or other disposition (or agreement as to the same) (b) Delivery or transfer (c) Ordinary course of business	Good faith and without notice

The effect in each case is that the buyer takes the property free of any particular defects in the seller's title at all, not free from all defects altogether. As Lord Goff explained in *National Employers' Mutual General Insurance Association Ltd v Jones* [1990] 1 AC 24, 58–59, the Factors Acts were:

> directed to giving protection to those who had dealt in good faith with factors or agents, to whom goods, or documents of title to goods, had been entrusted, to the extent that the rights of such persons should (so far as provided) override those of the owner who had so entrusted the goods or documents to the factor or agent. There is not the slightest indication in the statute that it was intended to take so radical a step as to depart (except in the limited circumstances I have indicated) from the cardinal principle of the law of property in chattels embodied in the Latin maxim *nemo dat quod non habet*, so as to enable a factor or agent, entrusted with goods by a thief or a purchaser from a thief, to give a good title to a bona fide purchaser from him, overriding the title of the true owner.

Unsurprisingly, given the seller and buyer in possession exceptions were introduced to consolidate the mercantile agent exception, there is a considerable amount of overlap between these provisions. But there are also some important distinctions. The detail is explored below, by reference to each of the three columns above.

(1) *Seller.* Under s 2, the seller must be a mercantile agent. That is defined in s 1 as someone who 'in the customary course of his business as such agent authority either to sell goods, or to consign goods for the purpose of sale, or to buy goods, or to raise money on the security of goods'. This describes the business of a nineteenth-century factor, but obviously can correspond to that of other commercial parties too. Indeed, the exception can apply even if the mercantile agent only acts for one principal, so long as the agent retains their 'independent middleman' status: *Lowther v Harris* [1927] 1 KB 393, 398 (per Wright J).

The seller must also be in possession of the goods or documents of title (the latter being given a wide definition in s 1 to include any document 'used in the ordinary course of business as proof of the possession or control of goods'). That possession must be in the seller's capacity as mercantile agent, and with the owner's consent, even if turns out that that consent was induced by fraud: *Pearson v Rose & Young* [1951] 1 KB 275. Denning LJ explained at 286–87, by the owner objectively consenting to someone else possessing goods or documents of title in their capacity as such: 'he has clothed the agent with apparent authority to sell them; and he should not therefore be allowed to claim them back from an innocent purchaser'. But this exposes the point that s 2 is entirely unnecessary: the work could be done through orthodox agency principles, without the need for a distinct statutory provision (see in this respect *Pickering v Busk* (1812) 15 East 38).

Section 8 was added because the Court of Appeal held in *Johnson v The Crédit Lyonnais Co* (1877) 3 CPD 32 (CA) that a tobacco broker and mercantile agent, having sold tobacco once but retained possession of them with the consent of the buyer, ceased holding the goods in its capacity as a mercantile agent. It followed that, when the tobacco broker then pledged some of those same goods to a bank to obtain credit, the pledge could not fall within the initial statutory mercantile agent exception. That in itself would not have been problematic had the Court of Appeal not *also* concluded that the broker lacked apparent authority at common law, based on an unconvincing distinction with *Pickering v Busk* and similar cases. The better view is that either agency or estoppel ought to have validated the tobacco broker's pledge in *Johnson*.

Section 8 applies to 'a person [who], having sold goods, *continues, or is*, in possession of the goods or of the documents of title to the goods' (emphasis added). In *Pacific Motor Auctions Pty v Motor Credits (Hire Finance) Ltd* [1965] AC 867, the Privy Council held that s 8 was designed to protect a buyer who would not be aware of a change in the capacity of the seller from mercantile agent to pure seller, and therefore the capacity in which the goods were possessed by the seller did not matter. Placing greater weight on 'continues' rather than 'or is', Lord Pearce held that the critical point was that, once the seller was in possession of the goods, there could be no subsequent break in the physical possession of the goods. The effect of this, as Lord Denning MR later said in *Worcester Works Finance Ltd v Cooden Engineering Co Ltd v Cooden Engineering Co Ltd* [1972] 1 QB 210, 217, is that the 'only relevant word is therefore "continues"'. Although the *Pacific Motors* decision is controversial (see Merrett 2008, 384–88), it can be supported on an orthodox agency or estoppel analysis: a change in capacity unknown to the buyer should not make difference on questions of apparent authority or apparent ownership. As Lord Pearce asked rhetorically at 886:

> The object of the section is to protect an innocent purchaser who is deceived by the vendor's physical possession of goods or documents and who is inevitably unaware of legal rights which fetter the apparent power to dispose. Where

a vendor retains uninterrupted physical possession of the goods why should an unknown arrangement, which substitutes a bailment for ownership, disentitle the innocent purchaser to protection from a danger which is just as great as that from which the section is admittedly intended to protect him?

A physical break in possession is an outwardly visible act which might put the buyer on notice that the seller cannot properly sell title to the goods. But this will depend on the facts of each case. So *Pacific Motors* goes too far in ruling that such a break will *always* take a transaction outside s 8. If it does not act to put the buyer on notice of the seller's lack of authority, it should not.

Section 9 applies to a buyer who has not (yet) acquired the interest which it has then purported to sell on to a subsequent purchaser. That may be because the transfer of title is contingent on payment, which has not yet been made, or where the subsequent purchaser is seeking to assert priority over some prior security interest. Like s 8, s 9 was adopted when the courts began to take a narrow approach to the mercantile agent exception. Like s 2, but unlike s 8, the buyer must be in possession with the consent of the relevant prior interest holder, and possession must in the buyer's capacity as such: *Fadallah v Pollak* [2013] EWHC 3159 (QB) at [55]–[56] (per HHJ Seymour QC).

(2) *Transaction.* Each of ss 2, 8 and 9 of the Factors Act 1889 requires a transaction. A sale is defined in familiar terms in s 2 of the Sale of Goods Act 1979 and a pledge is discussed at page 136 below. In *Worcester Works*, Megaw and Phillimore LJJ held (at 218–20) that 'other disposition' requires some transfer of an interest in goods. Lord Denning suggested (at 218) that it extended to the creation of new interests too, but that point has not yet been tested in subsequent litigation.

The requirement for the transaction to place in the ordinary course of business is perhaps less straightforward. It does not arise for s 8. It appears on the face of s 2 of the 1889 Act but not on the face of s 9. However, in *Newtons of Wembley Ltd v Williams* [1965] 1 QB 560, it was held that the words in s 9 'shall have the same effect as if the person making the delivery or transfer were a mercantile agent …', effectively incorporated the ordinary course of business requirement. This is dubious. The better construction, taken in Australia and New Zealand, is that those words import no further requirement, and English courts have subsequently indicated that if not bound by *Newtons*, they might take a similar line: see *Forsythe International (UK) Ltd v Silver Shipping Co Ltd*

[1994] 1 WLR 1334, 1351 (per Clarke J). In any event, it is not clear what the requirement of ordinary course of business adds to lack of notice. The two requirements seem to be entirely duplicative. As Buckley LJ made clear in *Oppenheimer v Attenborough & Sons* [1908] 1 KB 221, 230–31, this requires the transaction to take place:

> within business hours, at a proper place of business, and in other respects in the ordinary way in which a mercantile agent would act, so that there is nothing to lead the pledgee to suppose that anything wrong is being done, or to give him notice that the disposition is one which the mercantile agent had no authority to make.

Sections 8 and 9, but not s 2, also require there to be delivery of the goods or transfer of the documents of title and provide that it is the delivery or transfer (not the sale, pledge or other disposition) that is treated as authorised. On the other hand, they also permit an agreement as to a sale, pledge or other disposition to suffice, unlike s 2, which actually requires sale, pledge or other disposition. It is not clear what purpose these distinctions serve. In any event, delivery has the same meaning here as in wider property law (see page 22 above) and can be actual or constructive. In *Michael Gerson (Leasing) Ltd v Wilkinson* [2001] QB 514 at [28], Clarke LJ held that it sufficed simply for there to be 'a change in the character of the seller's possession' by the seller acknowledging that it was now holding on account as bailee for the buyer.

(3) *Buyer*. The position of the buyer is relatively straightforward and the requirements are the same for all three sections. Although the 1889 Act does not define good faith, it probably means no more than honesty: s 61(3) of the Sale of Goods Act 1979. Notice requires either the buyer actually to be aware of a lack of title or authority on the part of the seller or wilfully shutting his eyes to the obvious: *Worcester Works* at 218 (per Lord Denning MR). An example is *Summers v Havard* [2011] 2 Lloyd's Rep 283, where the buyer knew the seller was 'up to "skulduggery"' and 'deliberately refrained from making enquiries' (at [15]–[16], per Arden LJ).

Anything more than this would impose an obligation of constructive notice, and would involve the court asking what enquiries reasonably ought to have been taken, and what they would have revealed. This would be broader than what is required when dealing with agents at common law. There is a policy reason for not taking such a broad approach. There 'is a desire to permit business to be conducted expeditiously without time-consuming enquiries' (Bridge 2019b, 266). Indeed, constructive notice would be inconsistent with the stated purpose of statutory intervention, which was to change the approach taken in the common law of agency in favour of the transaction principle. In that context, it would make no sense to have a more onerous requirement for notice under the 1889 Act than at common law.

As can be seen, the Factors Act exceptions were responsive to historical commercial concerns that have fallen away and are in any event encrusted with technical and unmeritorious distinctions. They represent a messy compromise between the property principle and the transaction principle and, like many compromises, satisfy no one. They are also unnecessary given subsequent developments at common law: it would be much better if they were abolished, and the balance between the property principle and the transaction principle left to the common law principles of apparent authority and apparent ownership.

4. APPLICATION OF THE PROPERTY PRINCIPLE TO DEBTS

Just as with land and chattels, there can be competing titles to debts; defects in title to the debt inherited by the assignee; and limitations in title preventing dealings with the debt. Underpinning many of these rules, once again, is the *nemo dat* or property principle.

The common law approach to debts – negotiability – suppressed these complexities by creating a clean title in the instrument when the transferee takes it in good faith and for value. As discussed in chapter two, that is an exception to *nemo dat* developed for policy reasons to encourage the currency of those particular forms of debts used as payment mechanism themselves.

However, when a debt is instead dealt with by way of equitable or statutory assignment, *nemo dat* and related issues cannot be avoided. That is true whichever of the models of assignment discussed in chapter two is adopted. Under the *transfer model*, the assignee takes the title of the assignor, 'warts and all'. And as for the *trust model*, the assignor can only create a bare trust over the rights he has. The assignee's new title is derivative on the existing title of assignor, and cannot better it. To stretch the analogy, the 'warts' still exist, but one stage removed from the assignee. *Barbados Trust Co Ltd v Bank of Zambia* [2007] EWCA Civ 148 is a case in point. An assignee, Bank of America, purported to declare a trust over a debt assigned to it. A majority held (Waller LJ dissenting) that the prior assignment to Bank of America had taken place in breach of a clause restricting assignment, and so was void. That meant that the bank had no contractual rights to hold on trust for vulture fund, so the trust was also void.

PRIORITY DISPUTES

In the law of assignment, title disputes are generally portrayed in terms of 'priority rules' where the creditor purports to assign the same debt twice to two different assignees. The question is: as between the two assignees, which title, in relative terms, is better? The answer depends on whether the assignments are by statute or in equity.

(1) *Priority between two equitable assignments.* The first scenario arises where the two assignments, *both* taking effect only in equity. The 'first to give notice' priority rule applies here: *Dearle v Hall* (1828) 3 Russ 1. In that case, a beneficiary under a trust assigned his trust income to Mr Dearle in 1808, Mr Sherring in 1809 and then Mr Hall in 1812. Neither Dearle nor Sherring gave notice to the trustees, but Hall did. Despite being last in time, Sir Thomas Plumer MR held that Hall was entitled to the income because he had been the first to give notice. The Master of the Rolls obviously struggled with the case, because he called the parties back to argue it a second time, and his grasp of the relevant principles was weak in his judgment. In particular, he ruled that assignment in equity does not 'attach' to the intangible property until notice to the obligor is given. That was wrong on the law at the time and remains wrong on the law now. Equitable assignment does not require notice to take effect: *Ward v Duncombe* [1893] AC 369, 391–92 (per Lord Macnaghten). Despite this fundamental error in the reasoning, the rule arising from *Dearle v Hall* itself has not been overturned.

On the transfer model of equitable assignment, *Dearle v Hall* is inexplicable without treating it as an exception to the *nemo dat* principle. It is, however, conceptually possible to reconcile it with *nemo dat* under the trust model of equitable assignment. Each assignment creates a fresh equitable right held by the assignee against debt held at law by assignor. A priority rule is needed to determine the relative strength of those competing titles (Fox 2006, 354). It is perfectly possible to adopt a 'first to give notice' priority rule instead of 'first in time'. Of course, that leaves the question: *why* should the law depart from the usual first in time rule?

Sir Thomas Plumer suggested in *Dearle v Hall* itself that the rule was justified because the first assignee, by not giving notice to the debtor, enabled the second assignment to take place. This is obviously a bad point. *First*, the notice does not have to be given by the assignee; it suffices that notice is given of the assignment by someone to the debtor. *Second*, in most cases, notice would not make any difference to a determined rogue. Notice does not have to be given in such a way as to make the second assignee aware of it. Indeed, in the absence of some public register, the second assignee is unlikely to know anything about the first assignment by reason of the notice unless a question is actually asked of the debtor. Even then the debtor is not obliged to tell the second assignee anything about the first assignment. *Third*, the first assignee is under no duty to give notice and cannot be said to have done anything wrong by not giving notice. It therefore seems harsh to make the assignee suffer the consequences of the duplicative assignment.

A second justification is that *Dearle v Hall* requires some publicity of what otherwise is a private transaction, and thereby brings some objective certainty to the question of who is entitled to payment of the debt (De Lacy 1999, 323). This is also unconvincing because the notice does not have to be in writing, need not specify to whom the debt must be paid, and need not be given to the other assignees. Nor is the debtor under a duty to tell the other assignees, even if asked (Oditah 1989, 525–27). In any event, any practical advantage gained from the rule in *Dearle v Hall* is undoubtedly outweighed by its practical disadvantages, including the great barrier it places in the way of efficient bulk assignments (for example, for receivables financing).

A third set of justifications argue that giving notice improves an assignee's equities (Tham 2019, 209–12) or is necessary to bind the conscience of the debtor and so trigger equity's full set of remedies in support of the assignment (Tolhurst 2002, 82–83). Tolhurst's argument might be called a 'perfection' or 'attachment' argument: it suggests that an assignment is not complete until notice is given. But that aspect of *Dearle v Hall* was rejected in *Ward v Duncombe*, and is clearly not good law. As for Tham, he bases his equities argument in large part on the 'potential' benefit to later assignees by 'modest' publicity created by giving notice. That simply takes us back to the first and second justifications we have already considered and rejected as unconvincing.

Dissatisfaction with the rule in *Dearle v Hall* has led to a number of judges suggesting it be disapplied in favour of the 'first in time' rule in certain circumstances. Four exceptions have been developed. *First*, the 'first to give notice' rule should only benefit an assignment for value as opposed to a voluntary assignment: *United Bank of Kuwait plc v Sahib* [1997] Ch 107, 119 (per Chadwick J). *Second*, the assignee benefitting from the 'first to give notice' rule must have acted in good faith and not had notice of the prior assignment when giving notice himself: *Ward v Duncombe* at 384 (per Lord Macnaghten). *Third*, the debtor cannot have learned about the earlier assignment: *Re Dallas* [1904] 2 Ch 385, 399 (per Buller J). *Fourth*, where no notice is given, the law defaults make to the 'first in time' rule.

Some commentators have, very fairly, made the point that the doctrinal foundations of these exceptions are not especially strong (De Lacy 1999, 315–22; Tham 2019, 219–34). But that misses the deeper point: the judicial desire to create exceptions to the rule in *Dearle v Hall* show that there is something wrong with the 'first to give notice' rule itself.

(2) *Priority between two statutory assignments.* The second scenario arises where there are two assignments, *both* of which are purportedly under s 136 of the Law of Property Act 1925. The transfer model should resolve the answer in favour of the first assignee. If title to the debt has been transferred once, the assignor has nothing left to transfer on the second occasion: *Cronk v McManus* (1892) 8 TLR 449. The second assignment is a nullity. This 'first in time' outcome reflects the *nemo dat* principle in operation.

Regrettably, this has been called into doubt by two cases preferring the 'first to give notice' priority rule developed in *Dearle v Hall*. These are *E Pfeiffer Weinkellerei-Weineinkauf GmbH & Co v Arbuthnot Factors Ltd* [1988] 1 WLR 150 and *Compaq Computer Ltd v Abercorn Group Ltd* [1991] BCC 484.

In practice, however, the application of the different priority rule makes no difference in this scenario. Notice will, by definition, have been given to the debtor for the first assignment. Nonetheless, as a matter of principle, *Pfeiffer* and *Compaq* should not be regarded as overruling

Cronk, which was not drawn to the attention of the court in either case. Importantly, both cases were considering the position where the first assignment was in equity, and the second was by way of statute (which is the fourth scenario below), and so are distinguishable.

(3) *Priority between two assignments, one in equity and one statutory.* A third scenario arises where the *first* assignment was under s 136 and the *second* was in equity. The first assignment will obviously prevail. The same outcome is achieved no matter whether the 'first in time' or 'first to give notice' rule applies, since the first assignment by definition will have required notice. The same outcome is also reached no matter whether the trust or transfer model is used to analyse the equitable assignment: after the transfer of the debt by the legal assignment, there is nothing left either to transfer or over which to declare a trust.

The final scenario is where the *first* assignment was in equity and the *second* was under s 136. There is some authority which suggests that the 'first in time' rule ought to be applied, subject to the second assignee establishing that he was a good faith purchaser for value: see, for example, *Performing Right Society Ltd v London Theatre of Varieties Ltd* [1924] AC 1, 19. However, that argument was rejected in *Pfeiffer Weinkellerei-Weineinkauf* and *Compaq Computer*. The reasoning in both cases (i) proceeds on the incorrect basis that s 136 simply implemented procedural changes to equitable assignment (contrast the discussion in chapter two above), (ii) was *obiter dicta* and (iii) in any event runs against the wider trend in the authorities by carving out exceptions to the rule in *Dearle v Hall* to limit its effect. Regrettably, however, *Pfeiffer* and *Compaq* remain the last word on this point.

SUBJECT TO EQUITIES

The property principle or *nemo dat* means that, if the assignor's right to payment is defective in some way, the assignee will take the debt with those same defects. The assignor cannot transfer the debt free of those defects Often this is expressed in the old-fashioned language of the assignee taking 'subject to equities': see, for example, s 136 itself, quoted at page 38 above.

There is limited difference between statutory and equitable assignment for these purposes. It is obviously regrettable that s 136 does not provide that a statutory assignment for value will overreach any equitable interests in the debt in the same way as a good faith purchaser for value of other forms of property. Elsewhere this forms a valuable function in cleaning title and making the property more marketable in the future. This is a straightforward and obviously beneficial reform that could be made to the law of assignment that would strike a better balance between the property and transaction principles.

If a debt is assigned from A to B to C, the only equities which count against C are those of A not B. This may be the law's attempt to limit the number of barnacles fastening to the debt in the absence of the good faith purchaser cleaning mechanism. On its face it appears to be contrary to *nemo dat* because C ends up with a better title than B (Tettenborn 2002, 491). But it makes sense for equitable assignment, at least, when that form of assignment is viewed through the prism of the trust model. That is because A is a bare trustee and C's claim must be in A's name not B's. However, this rule has been read over to s 136 when it need not be: it is another casualty of treating statutory assignment as merely tinkering at the procedural edges of equitable assignment, rather than creating a different model of assignment.

It is convenient at this point to distinguish between two categories of equities. The *first* category arises where the contract by which the debt has been created is defective in some way. For example, the contract may be unenforceable for illegality; it cannot become enforceable once the right to payment is assigned to a third party, even if the third party knows nothing of the illegality. Similarly, the debtor may be able to rescind the contract because it was procured by misrepresentation, duress or undue influence. The 'mere equity' or 'power' to rescind remains attached to the debt even as it is transferred under s 136 or made the subject of a bare trust via equitable assignment. This is a variation of the same principle we discussed in the context of sale of goods at page 77 above.

The *second* category arises where the debtor has a counterclaim against the assignor. In some circumstances the debtor can set-off, that is, reduce, his debt against the assignee by reference to that cross-claim against the assignor. That is because *nemo dat* requires that the assignor cannot give the assignee the benefit of the debt without the effect of set-off. These rules are complex and developed before the introduction of statutory assignment, when the action was always in the name of the assignor. That may make some sense of them – although that is far from a justification for them.

Different types of set-off interact with assignment in different ways and for different reasons. There are four types of set-off (though see Wood 1989, 6–12).

(1) *Procedural set-off.* This label groups together the continuing effect of the Statutes of Set-Off (the Insolvent Debtors Relief Act 1729 and the Debtors Relief Amendment Act 1935), despite their repeal, and the Statutes' analogous application in equity. Wood calls this 'independent set-off', and that terminology has been adopted in some of the more recent cases. Procedural or independent set-off does not take effect until judgment. The cross-claim must be for a debt that is due before the claim for the debt was issued but need not to have any connection to (and so be 'independent of') the claimed debt. On judgment, the claim and cross-claim are 'merged' into the judgment to create a single net liability.

The *nemo dat* principle means that assignment of a debt after judgment on litigation where there is a cross-claim can only be of the reduced judgment debt (if the cross-claim was less than the claim) or no debt at all (if the cross-claim was equal to or greater than the cross-claim). Further, where a debt is assigned before judgment, the assignee remains at risk of the set-off unless he gives notice before a debt has accrued that can be cross-claimed.

It is difficult to justify that rule as being about title to the debt. The better justification is giving procedural protection to the debtor. As Lord Mansfield recognised in *Green v Farmer* (1768) 4 Burr 820, procedural set-off was developed to promote judicial economy, by encouraging two parties to settle their differences at once. The introduction of a third person, the assignee, signals an end to that possibility but, in order to give the debtor some certainty, the set-off only comes to an end on notice of the assignment rather than on the assignment itself. Until notice is given, the debtor can continue to accrue set-offs against the assignor.

(2) *Transaction set-off.* In contrast, transaction set-off is substantive and, once asserted, can take effect outside the confines of litigation procedures. Wood developed this term to cover common law abatement and another form of equitable set-off, which was developed to mitigate the rigours of abatement and has now largely swallowed it up. These are the most significant set-offs in commercial practice.

Abatement allows a debtor under a contract for the sale of goods or services to reduce the debt by reference to the damages arising from the creditor's breach of the same contract when providing those goods and services. Equitable set-off was developed to widen abatement, albeit still limited to the contracts which constitute the relevant transaction. It takes effect where the cross-claim is 'closely connected' to the claim such that it would be 'manifestly unjust' to enforce the debt without enforcing the cross-claim: *Geldof Metaalconstructie NV v Simon Carves Ltd* [2010] EWCA Civ 667, at [42] (per Rix LJ). It has been emphasised that this involves discretion based on the justice of the case: *Bibby Factors Northwest Ltd v HDF Ltd* [2015] EWCA Civ 1908, at [48] (per Christopher Clarke LJ). So this involves something of a value judgement. There will be difficult cases at the margins where judges will reach different conclusions, such as where dealings between the parties could fairly be characterised as either a single course of transacting or a series of discrete transactions.

Assignees are always vulnerable to substantive set-off arising from the debtor's cross-claim. Giving notice has no effect. This has traditionally been explained in the language of 'impeaching title', which Rix LJ in *Geldof* dismissed at [43] as 'an unhelpful metaphor in the modern world'. It is certainly no good as the *test* for transaction set-off; but title does provide an underlying *explanation* for the rule. It reflects the fact that the debt was always at risk of being reduced or extinguished by transaction set-off, and, by reason of *nemo dat*, the assignor cannot transfer or create a trust conferring a better title than the one they originally had.

This justification is criticised on the basis that the cross-claim may only arise after the assignment, so it cannot be described as a flawed asset at the time of transfer (Tettenborn 2002, 487–88). But the point is that transaction set-off is in prospect (albeit inchoate) at the time of assignment. Put another way, there is a 'power' or 'mere equity' of transaction set-off in the same way as there might be a power or mere equity in a voidable contract at the assignment. If we are comfortable treating the latter as an instance of *nemo dat* (see pages 77 and 94 above), why not the former?

(3) *Contractual set-off.* The parties can agree to enlarge or restrict the rules of procedural and transaction set-off, and when they do the assignees will be bound by those agreements. Again, this is the *nemo dat* principle in operation: the assignor can only give the assignee what he had to begin with.

Parties often expressly agree enlarged set-off (or similar) arrangements in order mitigate against credit risk, and limit their exposure to the possibility of insolvency. This is sometimes called netting, to reflect the idea that the parties have agreed to consolidate the payment obligations owed each way to a single, net balance. We will discuss this further in the context of credit risk at pages 130–31 below. In contrast, where the cash flow is important, or where parties wish to facilitate dealings in the debt, they will expressly agree to exclude set-off to ensure it cannot be used to avoid prompt payment. Set-off by agreements can also often be implied, either in fact on the basis of business efficacy or in law to reflect market standard practices and customs. For example, if a bank customer has multiple current accounts, the bank has the benefit of implied term entitling it to combine those accounts. Set-off can also be impliedly excluded where liquidity is important. So, for example, set-off has been excluded from payment instruments and obligations to pay freight for the carriage of cargo.

In *Gilbert Ash (Northern) Ltd v Modern Engineering (Bristol) Ltd* [1974] AC 689, Lord Diplock held (at 717) that there was a presumption against parties excluding set-off; 'clear express words' must be used to rebut that presumption. Not only is that contrary to the examples just given, it is clearly wrong as a matter of principle. There are often perfectly valid reasons why parties might have wanted to exclude set-off without having expressly said as much, including where it is reasonably in contemplation that the debt may be dealt with as a commodity. Additional obstacles should not therefore be put in the way of an implied exclusion of set-off.

(4) *Insolvency set-off.* Finally, when a debtor goes into administration or liquidation (concepts explained further in chapter six) a set-off is executed between the debtor and its creditors to the extent that its creditors also owe money to the now-insolvent debtor. These are mandatory rules now found in the Insolvency Act 1986 (s 323) and the Insolvency Rules 2016 (rules 14.24–14.25). They cannot be enlarged or restricted by contract. The existence of this set-off, and the rule that it cannot be excluded by contract, is difficult to justify but space precludes further discussion here.

For present purposes, it suffices to note the interaction of assignment with insolvency set-off. Insolvency set-off will be executed as between debtor and assignee; it will not be executed as between debtor and assignor, even if no notice of the assignment is given to the debtor. This is nothing to do with *nemo dat* but instead reflects the (questionable) policy behind insolvency set-off, which is to avoid a perceived unfairness of a creditor paying the estate the debt it owed in full and then only receiving a fraction of the debt due to it in return (Wood 1989, 271). That policy applies regardless of how it has come to be that the creditor has a claim against the estate.

CONTRACTUAL PROHIBITIONS ON ASSIGNMENT

The assignability of the title to the debt may be inherently limited by the terms of the debt itself. Not infrequently parties include clauses in contracts along the following lines: 'No party shall without the written consent of the other party assign any rights under this contract.'

In *Linden Garden Trust Ltd v Lenesta Sludge Disposal Ltd* [1994] 1 AC 85, the House of Lords held that a clause in this form would prevent the assignment of debts accruing under the same contract. Lord Browne-Wilkinson emphasised there was no public policy or commercial objection to that outcome; indeed, freedom of contract demanded that effect be given to the clause, and the parties themselves best placed to judge the commerciality of their arrangements.

Linden Garden has attracted a furious debate. Objections to non-assignment clauses preventing transfers of contractual rights fall into two groups.

First, there are objections from principle. For example, Goode has argued that, as a matter of contractual analysis, a breach of a non-assignment clause should not do more than qualify the debtor's duties to any assignee; the contractual term cannot nullify the transfer of the chose in action itself (2009, 303–06). While that argument recently attracted judicial approval in *First Abu Dhabi Bank PJSC v BP Oil International Ltd* [2018] EWCA Civ 14, there are difficulties with it as a matter of principle. The content of a contractual term turns on its proper interpretation. It is artificial to interpret the typical non-assignment clause in the way proposed by Goode. Treating a contractual right subject to a non-assignment clause as non-alienable shows greater fidelity to the agreement struck between the parties. The proprietary perspective adopted when considering the position between assignor and assignee should not change the analysis. It is wrong to think of this in terms of freedom of contracting 'trumping' property (contrast Bridge 2016a, 59). An assignor cannot transfer what is not his to transfer. This is simply the *nemo dat* or property principle in action (Tolhurst and Carter 2014, 422–23; Turner 2008, 326–27). In any event, given that property is typically defined by reference to the ability to confer the right to the thing on another (as discussed in chapter one), the property objection becomes circular. This argument boils down to '"Property" is "property" because it is "property": property status and proprietary consequence confuse each other in a deadening embrace of cause and effect' (Gray 1991, 293). A further objection of principle focuses on equitable assignments. Since an equitable assignment does not involve the transfer of an existing right as between assignor and debtor but instead involves the creation of a new right as between assignor and assignee, it is questionable whether (i) normal assignment clauses focusing on transfer in fact apply as a matter of construction (Edelman and Elliott 2015, 249) and, (ii) if so, the debtor can contract to prevent something which does not, in law, concern him. The efficacy of a clause prohibiting the creation of a trust has not yet been tested properly in the authorities. In *Barbados Trust Co Ltd v Bank of Zambia* [2007] EWCA Civ 148, there was a clause banning assignment in similar terms to that set out above. To try to get around it, Bank of America declared a trust over the debt to a vulture fund and the vulture fund then attempted to sue the debtor using the *Vandepitte* procedure. The Court of Appeal accepted that a prohibition on assignment would not prohibit the creation of an express trust, and a majority (Hooper LJ dissenting) were in principle willing to allow the use of the *Vandepitte* procedure on the facts to bring the claim to evade the contractual prohibition on assignment. However, the Court of Appeal in *Barbados Trust* appeared to assume that an express prohibition on trust, had it been negotiated, would have been effective to preclude the creation of a trust. That may not be right, for the reasons already given, and more recently the Court of Appeal in *First Abu Dhabi* cast doubt on that proposition.

Second, there are objections from policy. The obviously-wrong argument that contractual rights are property rights, and property rights should be capable of alienation as a matter of policy, has given way to a more refined approach. It is now common ground that there are good commercial reasons for restricting assignment. The example normally given is that non-assignment clauses are essential to the effectiveness of certain types of contract, such as where mutual obligations are to be discharged by way of contractual netting. Contractual netting is commonplace in some financial markets, such as derivatives where the ISDA and other master agreements are routinely used by parties, in order to mitigate against credit risk (see further pages 130–31 below).

But the more fundamental point is that all debtors have perfectly legitimate reasons for controlling to whom they owe contractual debts. While debtors' prisons have been abolished, friendly creditors are much still to be preferred to hostile ones. So, for example, in *Barbados Trust*, the debtor found itself being pursued by an aggressive vulture fund when it had bargained for its loan facility being enforceable at the discretion of a bank or similarly more restrained financial institution. An even more stark example is *Fitzroy v Cave* [1905] 2 KB 364, where the assignee wanted to make the debtor bankrupt and force him out from the board of their company. He obtained the assignment of as many of the debtors' debts with that sole object in mind. The Court of Appeal, albeit with some reluctance, held there was nothing to stop the assignee in that course of action, even though he had no real interest in any actual proceeds from the assignment. If the claimant in *Fitzroy* had acquired rights to *damages* rather than debts, it is very likely that his campaign against the defendant would still be caught by the doctrine of maintenance, because it is difficult to say that the claimant had a 'genuine commercial interest' in the outcome of the litigation: *Trendtex Trading Corp v Credit Suisse* [1982] AC 679, 703 (per Lord Roskill). It is extraordinary that the law has abdicated any role in regulating this sort of malicious conduct when it comes to *debts* (see also MacMahon 2020, 310–12), but, given that it has, it is entirely understandable that debtors then want to guard against this sort of risk upfront through anti-assignment clauses in their contracts.

On the other hand, non-assignment clauses are recognised to create obstacles to receivables financing, also known as 'factoring'. As discussed at page 42 above, this is where a company assigns its book debts as they accrue to a financing party in exchange for credit. This is a particularly attractive financing option for smaller commercial enterprises, who can struggle to access other forms of lending. The effect of non-assignment clauses is to make its availability more difficult (Beale, Gullifer and Paterson, 2016). This has long been seen as a problem. In *Barbados Trust*, for example, Rix LJ said that 'it would be highly undesirable' if debtors could 'totally' prevent their suppliers from factoring by the use of non-assignment clauses (at [118]).

The apparent commercial attraction of factoring probably underpins the difficult case of *Foamcrete (UK) Ltd v Thrust Engineering Ltd* [2002] BCC 221. In that case, rather than the debt being created first and then assigned, the parties first entered into a security arrangement containing an agreement to assign, the scope of which extended to a debt later created but expressed to be non-assignable. The Court of Appeal held that the debt was assigned, since the reasoning in *Linden Garden* only applied to subsequent assignments. Not only is that a misreading of *Linden Garden* (Tettenborn 2010, 196–97), it ignores the point that there was no *scintilla temporis* between the creation of the debt and the ban on its assignment. The debt was created non-assignable, and it was therefore contrary to the *nemo dat* principle for it to be assigned. It can only be hoped that *Foamcrete* will be overturned when an appropriate case arises.

BUSINESS CONTRACT TERMS (ASSIGNMENT OF RECEIVABLES) REGULATIONS 2018

Beginning with the Uniform Commercial Code in the US, a number of jurisdictions have gradually 'banned the ban' and legislated against anti-assignment clauses with the aim of facilitating invoice factoring. The UK government followed this trend and decided the time had come to intervene in the law of assignment again: see Department for Business, Innovation and Skills 2014. Section 1 of the Small Business, Enterprise and Employment Act 2015 allowed regulations to be promulgated to render non-assignment clauses non-effective in whole or in part. On 23 November 2018, after lengthy and somewhat controversial consultations (Beale 2020, 123–36), the Business Contract Terms (Assignment of Receivables) Regulations 2018 came into force.

Regulation 2(1) contains the general prohibition on the effectiveness of non-assignment clauses in contracts entered into from 31 December 2018:

> a term in a contract has no effect to the extent that it prohibits or imposes a condition, or other restriction, on the assignment of a receivable arising under that contract or any other contract between the same parties.

A 'receivable' is defined as a right to be paid under a contract for the supply of goods, services or intangible assets. 'Assignment' is nowhere defined. However, given the Government's focus on encouraging factoring, it must extend to equitable assignment. Factoring is done by way of equitable assignment because giving notice to all of a company's debtors as they arise (as is required under statutory assignment) would be too onerous a task.

After the general prohibition, there follow two significant caveats. *First*, Regulation 3 provides that the general prohibition only applies where the supplier of goods, services or intangible assets is neither (i) 'special purpose vehicle' incurring a liability of £10 million or more or (ii) a 'large supplier', that is, companies and limited liability partnerships having two or more of the following characteristics at the time of assignment: (i) a turnover of not more than £36 million; (ii) a balance sheet of not more than £18 million; (iii) no more than 250 employees.

Second, Regulation 4 provides that various types of contracts are exempted from the general prohibition. Vast swathes of the domestic commercial contract eco-system are exempted, including: contracts concerned with interests in land; share and business sale agreements; various financial services contracts; options, futures, swaps and other derivatives contracts; and various types of contracts found in the energy market, such as those relating to petroleum licences.

The Regulations are, to a certain extent, to be welcomed. The question of whether non-assignment clauses should be overridden as a matter of policy cannot be answered in a vacuum. The balance of interests in any particular market and between different types of counterparty must be weighed. That is what the Regulations purport to do. Nonetheless, the presumption *against* freedom of contract (which was borrowed from the Uniform Commercial Code) is somewhat uncomfortable and may explain why there are so many carve outs to it. Indeed, one of the architects of the legislation describes the final result as 'profoundly unsatisfactory' (Beale 2020, 136–38), precisely because of the numerous exceptions. That has made the UK 'ban of the ban' much narrower than other systems, including compared to the US Uniform Commercial Code. Yet, even with those carve outs, the Regulations may still be said to be disproportionate, given the primary objective was to make receivables financing more accessible to small businesses (MacMahon 2020, 310). It would have been preferable had the Regulations started the other way around and confirmed that bans on assignments were effective with exceptions in certain circumstances where it was felt that they seriously impeded business access to financing by way of factoring.

5

Performance Risk

Performance risk is the risk which one party to a contract takes that the other party will keep their promise to perform. It is also the risk taken as to whether that performance is good enough for the purpose for which it was acquired. This chapter draws a distinction between performance risk that is 'quantitative' and that which is 'qualitative'. For example, in a contract for the supply of services, the person acquiring those services takes a risk that their counterparty may not provide those services (a quantitative risk), or that the quality of the services supplied are in some way deficient (a qualitative risk). Likewise, in a sales contract, the goods may not be delivered or title may not be transferred (quantitative); alternatively, while those quantitative promises are kept, the goods may not correspond with their description or sample, or may not be reasonably fit for the purpose for which they were bought (qualitative). These are different types of risk and lead to different types of remedies, including different monetary awards. For the purposes of this chapter, however, the assumption is that the party in default *will* pay such an award; the question of credit risk – and insolvency – is considered in the next chapter.

Commercial law has shifted over time from *caveat emptor* ('let the buyer beware') to *caveat venditor* ('let the seller beware'). That shift as to where performance risk should sit began at common law, was captured by Sir Mackenzie Chalmer's codification of the law of sales, and has been accelerated since by further statutory intervention, both by amending the sales legislation (now consolidated in the Sale of Goods Act 1979) and by introducing further legislation for other types of transactions (such as the Supply of Goods and Services Act 1982). (In this chapter, references to the 1979 Act are to the Sale of Goods Act 1979 and references to the 1982 Act are to the Supply of Goods and Services Act 1982.) This shift as to where performance risk sits has been driven by the development of terms implied in law and in custom. These contractual rights are not – or, at least, are no longer – implied as ad hoc gap fillers reflecting what the parties intended but did not state in express terms, but rather as *default rules* for contracts for the sale of goods and supply of services out of which the parties can contract if they so wish. So it is important to be clear at the outset that this shift as to where performance risk sits in any transaction in a commercial transaction from buyer beware to seller beware is merely as to the starting point; ultimately each case turns on what the parties choose to agree.

At the start of the eighteenth century, buyer protections in respect of performance risk were limited to breach of contract claims under express warranties and to tort claims in cases of fraud. The courts began to shift towards a more-buyer friendly regime in the eighteenth century and early nineteenth centuries when commercial contracts were brief, containing little more than the headline commercial terms. Judges justified the implication of terms on the basis that the parties must have intended to incorporate the usages of the markets in which they traded and sought to identify those usages with the benefit of mercantile juries. However, over time, written contractual terms became more comprehensive, modes of incorporation became more sophisticated and there has been increasing use of standard form terms which have less gaps to fill. This was driven by changes in commercial practice but also, at least in part, in order to control the implication of terms at law. Thus 'trading practices, drafting practices and the law governing the construction of contracts and the implication of terms developed hand in hand' (Mitchell 2020, 214).

1. QUANTITATIVE PERFORMANCE RISK

EXPRESS TERMS AND DEFAULT RIGHTS

The core quantitative rights in commercial contracts are often expressly stated. For example, a contract for the supply of services will identify in broad terms the type of services for which the payor is bargaining. The parties will look to the express terms to identify what services were supposed to be rendered. Likewise, a loan agreement will on its express terms disclose the amount of capital to be advanced. Without such headline commercial terms, the agreement may not be sufficiently complete to constitute a contract. However, the law adopts a relatively low threshold as to when a contract is sufficiently complete. Even some core quantitative rights can be left to the common law's default rules. For instance, if the parties leave unsaid the price for the goods or services, the law will imply a term that a 'reasonable price' be paid, with reasonableness to be treated as a question of fact dependent on the circumstances of the case: s 9 of the 1979 Act and s 15 of the 1982 Act.

We discussed at page 17 above that the transfer of ownership to goods is the essence of a sales contract. The law's default rule used to be that the seller was 'not liable for a bad title unless there was an express warranty': *Morley v Attenborough* (1849) 3 Exch 500, 512 (per Parke B). The starting point has now been reversed. Section 12(1) of the 1979 Act provides for an implied promise by sellers that they have the 'right to sell the goods' at the time of when title is to pass, and s 12(3) then envisages that this can be disapplied if the parties agree to the contrary (see, to similar effect, ss 2(1) and 11 of the 1982 Act).

This may be thought to mean that sellers will be in breach whenever they do not own the property being sold, albeit that there may no loss where a *nemo dat* 'exception' is engaged (as to which, see chapter four). The better view, however, is that there would be no breach where a *nemo dat* exception applies, although this only enjoys *obiter* support: *Niblett Ltd v Confectioners' Material Co Ltd* [1921] 3 KB 387, 401–02 (per Atkin LJ). What is clear, however, is that s 12(1) implies a term that goes *beyond* the question of ownership of the goods themselves. In *Niblett* itself, for example, there was no question that the seller owned the preserved milk being sold. However, there was a breach because the labels of the tins ('Nissly') infringed an existing trademark ('Nestlé') and so, to that extent, there was a 'title superior', as Atkin LJ put it (at 402) to part of what was being sold. Indeed, *Niblett* can be viewed as authority for an even wider construction of s 12(1). Scrutton LJ's test was that s 12(1) would be breached whenever 'a vendor can be stopped by process of law from selling' (at 398).

REMEDIES I: RESTITUTION AND DEBT

Where a party pays for goods or services, and they simply are not delivered or (in the case of goods) title is not transferred by the counterparty, that party is entitled to recover the money paid by a claim in unjust enrichment on the basis of failure of consideration. This recognises that the money was paid subject to an agreed condition of receiving the goods (and title to the goods) or services, and that condition has not materialised, so the money ought to be returned.

This was recognised in *Rowland v Divall* [1923] 2 KB 500, which we discussed at page 17 above, where the court dismissed an argument that there had been no failure of consideration in the context of the sales agreement because the claimant had nonetheless had the benefit of possessing the car for a couple of months. This can be contrasted with *Yeoman Credit Ltd v Apps* [1962] 2 QB 508, where the car was delivered under a hire purchase agreement. It was held there was no failure of consideration in that case because the hirer had had the benefit of using the car for six months. That reflects the difference in focus between a sales contract and a hire purchase agreement.

The outcome of *Rowland v Divall* has been criticised for conferring a windfall on the buyer for the few months of use before the transaction is unwound (Bridge 2019b, 212). A stark illustration of this is *Butterworth v Kingsway Motors Ltd* [1954] 1 WLR 1286, where the claimant had the free use of a car for nearly a year during which it depreciated as a capital asset by around a third, before then claiming back the purchase price. However, the answer to this injustice lies not in the exclusion of the restitution claim, but rather in the full use of the principle of counter-restitution. When a claim in unjust enrichment arises, just as the seller should give restitution of the purchase price, so too should the buyer give restitution of benefits derived from the transaction, to ensure *restitutio in integrum* (see, further, Burrows 2012, 569–72).

The opposite situation is where a party delivers goods or services on condition of being paid and is not paid: the creditor can bring a claim for the debt due. This is a claim at common law but has been partly codified by s 49 of the 1979 Act (also discussed at pages 21–22 above). The enforcement of this condition takes place in contract rather than unjust enrichment, but this shows that the distinction between contract claim and a claim in unjust enrichment for failure of consideration is a relatively thin one.

REMEDIES II: DAMAGES

It is also open to parties to sue for damages compensating for loss arising from breach of a quantitative obligation (although an election must be made between this and a claim in unjust enrichment). In the sales context, the seller can sue the buyer for damages for non-acceptance of the goods (s 50 of the 1979 Act) and the buyer can sue for damages for non-delivery of the goods (s 51 of the 1979 Act).

The compensation principle for damages has come under sustained attack in recent years. It has been argued that a core function of damages is not to compensate for loss but to act as a substitute for the contractual right to performance or performance itself (Stevens 2009; Winterton 2015). Another school of thought is that, in the specific context of commercial sales, the 'demands of certainty in trade outweigh any principle that claimants should receive individualised compensation' (Bridge 2016b, 412). However, in *Bunge SA v Nidera BV* [2015] 3 All ER 1082, Lord Sumption robustly reaffirmed the compensation principle, saying at [21]:

> Sections 50 and 51 of the Sale of Goods Act, like the corresponding principles of the common law, are concerned with the price of the goods or services which would have been delivered under the contract. They are not concerned with the value of the contract as an article of commerce in itself.

Damages compensate for loss caused by the breach that is not too remote. This can be broken down into three components:

(1) *Factual causation* usually involves the 'but for' test embedded in Parke B's famous formulation in *Robinson v Harman* (1848) 1 Ex 850, 855 that 'where a party sustains a loss by reason of a breach of contract, he is, so far as money can do it, to be placed in the same situation, with respect to damages, as if the contract had been performed'.

(2) *Legal causation* considers what actual gains or losses should be disregarded even if satisfying the 'but for' test. Often this is by the doctrine of mitigation. McGregor explained this as comprising (i) a duty on the claimant to take all reasonable steps to avoid loss consequent on the defendant's breach of contract, (ii) an entitlement to claim all losses so long as those reasonable steps have been taken and (iii) a rule against claiming avoided loss (see now Edelman, Varuhas and Colton 2020, 223–24). However, it is better understood as a rule that (i) if the claimant acted reasonably after breach they are entitled to claim all losses but (ii) if they did not act reasonably after breach then damages are to be assessed *as if* they had instead acted reasonably (Dyson and Kramer 2014, 263).

(3) *Remoteness* can act to further exclude losses. In *Hadley v Baxendale* (1854) 9 Ex 341, 355 Alderson B held that only (i) losses which arose

naturally or ordinarily from the breach of contract and (ii) losses in the reasonable contemplation of the parties at the time of contracting can be recovered. Limb (i) is actually an answer (but not the only one) to the question asked within limb (ii): the parties will have reasonably contemplated losses arising naturally or ordinarily from the breach of contract at the time of contracting (albeit they may reasonably have contemplated other losses too, depending on the facts). There is a debate about whether this is an external rule of law or a default rule about the scope of contractual duties that can change on the proper construction of the relevant contract (Kramer 2005). While *Transfield Shipping Inc v Mercator Shipping Inc (The Achilleas)* [2009] 1 AC 61 lends the default rule argument some support, it remains controversial. Space precludes further discussion here.

Once legal causation – including mitigation – and remoteness are properly factored into quantification of damages, many of the outcomes which otherwise look decidedly non-compensatory and provide grist to the mill for proponents of substitutive damages such as Stevens and Winterton, can instead be reconciled with the principle that contract damages are fundamentally a loss-based remedy. This emphasis on legal causation (and remoteness) is of more than just academic significance: in practice these doctrines significantly affect the defaulting party's exposure to performance risk.

Subsection (3) of each of ss 50 and 51 contains a rule that, if there is an available market for the goods in question, the measure of damages is normally the difference between the (i) contract price and (ii) the market price on the date that the goods were not accepted (under s 50) or not delivered (under s 51). This rule is simply a function of legal causation: the reasonable thing for a commercial party to do on the date that goods are not accepted or not delivered, if there is an available market, is to go into that market to sell those goods (under s 50) or buy substitute goods (under s 51). If that is what the claimant does, they can claim their actual loss. If they do not, their actual actions are ignored and their damages are instead calculated by reference to the market price *as if* they had gone into the market.

An example is *Campbell Mostyn (Provisions) Ltd v Barnett Trading Co* [1954] 1 Lloyd's Rep 65, which was a claim under s 50. This involved a contract for the sale of 350 cases of tinned ham shipped to England from South Africa. The buyers refused to accept delivery. The sellers were entitled to damages for their loss reflecting the difference between the contract price and the market price at the date of breach, even though after the date of breach there was a rise in the market price for tinned ham, and the buyers were able to sell the cases for a profit. That was because the appropriate act of mitigation would have been to sell the ham into the market immediately on the defendant's refusal to accept delivery, rather than holding on to see which way the market would go in the medium term. Having not taken that step, the claimant was to be treated as if they had. As Lord Toulson later explained in *Bunge v Nidera* at [80], '[t]he speculation which way the market will go is the speculation of the claimant', and so those consequences of non-performance cannot be visited on the defendant no matter whether it aggravates the loss or reduces it.

The same approach is taken under s 51, as seen in *William Bros v Ed T Agius Ltd* [1914] AC 510. There, a cargo of coal was not delivered to the claimant. The price for coal rose after the parties entered into the contract. A month before the date of delivery, the claimant then entered into a contract with a third party (a 'sub-sale'), the intention being to use the coal supplied by the defendant to perform the contract with the third party at a profit. In the intervening month, the price for coal rose further. The claimant was entitled to claim for the difference between the contract and the market price, rather than having its damages reduced by reference to the price achieved in the sub-sale. The defendant had had no knowledge of any sub-sale at the time of contracting, so the sub-sale could be regarded as too remote, or beyond the scope of duty properly construed. Further, the sub-sale did not *require* the claimant to use the defendant's coal as delivered to satisfy the third party contract; as a matter of mitigation the claimant would reasonably have to go into the market to buy substitute coal in light of the defendant's failure to perform.

Although it has been argued that this market rule is a 'hard rule' (Bridge 2016b, 407), it is only a default measure for compensating for non-performance and, in appropriate circumstances, there can be departures. In *R & H Hall Ltd v WH Pim Jnr & Co Ltd* (1928) 33 Com Cas 423, a sub-sale was brought into account to increase damages in a claim for non-delivery of a cargo of wheat. The critical differences from *Williams v Agius* were twofold: (i) the sub-sale to the third party was a 'string contract', that is, was an on-sale of the specific cargo which had been promised by the defendant, and so the claimant could not mitigate by going into the market to obtain a substitute, and (ii) the loss was not too remote because the terms of the contract between the claimant and the defendant expressly envisaged that string contracts could be entered into. So *Hall v Pim* can be justified on orthodox damages principles, even though it was said at the time to have been a decision which 'astonished the Temple and surprised St Mary Axe': *James Finlay & Co Ltd v NV Kwik Hoo Tang Handel Maatschappij* [1929] 1 KB 400, 417 (per Sankey LJ).

2. QUALITATIVE PERFORMANCE RISK

EXPRESS TERMS AND DEFAULT RIGHTS

Separately from the risk that parties do not perform their obligations at all, there is the risk that they do perform, but do so in some deficient way. This risk is borne by the party envisaged to receive the goods, services or credit, unless the contract expressly or impliedly shifts the risk to the counterparty. As discussed at pages 103–04 above, this risk has increasingly been transferred over time to the suppliers of the goods, services or credit as a result of implied terms and more detailed standard form contracts.

There are a number of ways in which qualitative performance risk can manifest itself. Some examples of the default rules that operate in this context are as follows:

(1) *Late performance.* An obvious example of a qualitative breach is where the goods, services or credit are delivered, but late. Normally this is determined by reference to some date in the express terms of the contract. Absent such an express term, however, performance is required on an implied basis to take place in a reasonable period of time: s 29(3) of the 1979 Act and s 14 of the 1982 Act. The question of reasonableness is determined by the court on the facts of the particular case. Additionally, in sales contracts, while the default position is that the seller must be ready and willing to deliver and the buyer must be ready and willing to pay the price, the time for payment of the price is not a condition save for, for perishable goods, where time of payment becomes a condition once notice of intention to re-sell is given: ss 10, 27, 28 and 48(3) of the 1979 Act.

(2) *Quality of the title and possession transferred.* A second example of qualitative risk is where title to property is transferred but that title is not what

the buyer expected. For example, the buyer may be surprised by finding that title is still subject to a third party security interest or that there is an operative RoT clause higher up in the chain of transactions. The default position is that this is not a risk which the buyer should take: s 12(2)(a) of the 1979 Act. However, the duty on the seller is a relatively low one; the security interest need only be disclosed or known about for it to be satisfied. This can therefore be viewed as an 'informational' duty on the seller, requiring the seller to be upfront about any defect in title in negotiations rather than hiding behind a *caveat emptor* principle (Hedley 2001).

A more onerous obligation on sellers is the default rule under s 12(2)(b) of the 1979 Act that:

> the buyer will enjoy quiet possession of the goods except so far as it may be disturbed by the owner or other persons entitled to the benefit of any charge or encumbrance so disclosed or known.

On the face of it, if A sold goods to B which were then stolen by C, B will have had his quiet possession disturbed, and A should be liable for breach of contract. That would plainly be an unworkable default rule, and so has been 'read down' to refer to third party rights that could come into existence in the future that would entitle the third party *lawfully* to interfere with possession of the property. But, even then, it does not seem fair that, as a default rule, A should be liable if he sells goods to B in circumstances where, many years later, C acquires rights that entitles him to take possession from B. Some form of 'cut off' is needed.

In *Microbeads AG v Vinhurst Road Markings* [1975] 1 WLR 218, where quiet possession was disturbed because a patent was granted after sale, Lord Denning MR rejected (at 223) any gloss that would further restrict section 12(2)(b). However, a more commercial approach was taken in *Athens Cape Naviera SA v Deutsche Dampfschiffahrts-Gesellschaft Hansa AG (The Barenbels)* [1985] 1 Lloyd's Rep 528, where an equivalent express term in a contract for the sale of a ship was construed as being limited to lawful interferences which arose from the facts *as they stood* at the time of delivery, even if the right to interfere had not yet accrued. It is possible to re-explain *Microbeads* on this basis, given the application for the patent had already been filed at the time of sale.

(3) *Consistency with description or sample*. As a default rule, the seller is responsible for ensuring that the property delivered or services rendered should be consistent with any prior description or sample given. Again,

the law is most developed in the context of sales of goods, but they reflect general contractual principles.

A fairly broad approach is taken to what is meant by 'sale by description' under the s 13 of the 1979 Act. By definition it applies to all sales in unascertained goods, and it also usually to sales for specific goods. The description need not be written or oral; it can be a description implied from the circumstances. To give a well-known but non-commercial example, in *Grant v Australian Knitting Mills Ltd* [1936] AC 85, the Privy Council held that the sale of woollen underwear displayed in a shop constituted sale by description. There is considerable overlap between this and a sale by sample under s 15, where the proffering of the sample amounts to a 'mute description' (Bridge 2019b, 462) of the goods that will be sold.

The performance risk on the seller for this form of qualitative breach was at one stage very high. In *FW Moore & Co v Landauer & So* [1921] 2 KB 519, a strong Court of Appeal (Bankes, Scrutton and Atkin LJJ) held the seller liable where the contract required delivery of canned fruit in cases of 30 cans and half had been tendered for delivery in cases of 24 cans, even though this made no difference in terms of the market value of the delivery. When elevated to the House of Lords, Lord Atkin continued this unattractive approach in *Arcos Ltd v EA Ronaasen & Son* [1933] AC 470, where staves were delivered to be manufactured into barrels which did not comply with the measurements in the contract. Lord Atkin recognised an exception for 'microscopic deviations' (at 479) but held that there was a breach even though the timber's deviations from the specification did not affect the ability to manufacture barrels.

Later cases have since sought to re-balance the performance risk as between buyer and seller in two ways. *First*, a distinction has been drawn in the cases between general descriptions and specific descriptions. Where the words were used to identify the kind of goods to be supplied in general terms rather than specific descriptions (such as weight and measurements), the test for compliance is a 'broader, more common-sense test of mercantile character', which involves standing back and asking whether that goods of that kind have in fact been delivered: *Ashington Piggeries Ltd v Christopher Hill Ltd* [1972] AC 441, 489 (per Lord Wilberforce).

Second, in *Reardon Smith Line Ltd v Hansen-Tangen* [1976] 1 WLR 989, Lord Wilberforce criticised *Moore v Landauer* as 'excessively technical and due for fresh consideration' and held that a description for these purposes should be limited to those things that constituted 'a substantial ingredient of the "identity" of the thing sold' (at 998). That claim concerned the construction and delivery of a ship. The claim was brought on the basis that the ship had been built at a different shipyard to the one specified in the contract. While that was a breach of a specific description, the claim was nonetheless dismissed because that was not a sufficiently important part of the identity of the ship. This has since become something like a test for reliance; the question is whether the relevant part of the description had 'sufficient influence in the sale to become an essential term of the contract': *Harlingdon & Leinster Enterprises Ltd v Christopher Hull Fine Art Ltd* [1991] 1 QB 564, 574 (per Nourse LJ).

This rebalancing brings sale by description back into line with the approach taken for sample sales, where the description generated by the sample has always been limited to what the sample would be reasonably relied upon to demonstrate in terms of quality. As Lord Macnaghten sensibly said in *James Drummond & Sons v EH Van Ingen & Co* (1887) 12 App Cas 284, at 297 that, although the 'sample speaks for itself', it

> cannot be treated as saying more than such a sample would tell a merchant of the class to which the buyer belongs, using due care and diligence, and appealing to it in the ordinary way and with the knowledge possessed by merchants of that class at the time. No doubt the sample might be made to say a great deal more. Pulled to pieces and examined by unusual tests which curiosity or suspicion might suggest, it would doubtless reveal every secret of its construction. But that is not the way in which business is done in this country.

(4) *Satisfactory quality*. Goods delivered must be of satisfactory quality: s 14(2) of the 1979 Act. No parallel default rule exists for services for reasons which are not clear, although services rendered must of course be carried out with reasonable care and skill: s 13 of the 1982 Act.

As with s 12(2), this could be regarded as an 'informational' duty since no contractual liability applies (i) to matters drawn to the buyer's attention before contracting or (ii) where the buyer carried out an examination which ought reasonably to have revealed the point: s 14(2C). This was considered in a consumer case, *Bramhill v Edwards* [2004] EWCA Civ 403. There, a couple bought a second-hand motor home which had been manufactured in the US and was two inches too wide for UK roads. The Court of Appeal considered that there had been no breach of s 14(2) but, if there had been, there was a defence under s 14(2C), because the buyers had spent a few days living in the motor home before buying it. The Court was also attracted by the argument that the seller had made a representation about the internal width of the motor home which should have alerted the buyers about the external width of the motor home. This decision has been criticised on the basis that the statutory informational duty is more exacting than that (Twigg-Flesner 2005): under limb (i) the relevant matter must be 'specifically' drawn to the buyer's attention (which it was not) and under limb (ii) the focus is on the examination which took place not the examination which could reasonably have taken place. These criticisms have force as a matter of statutory interpretation, but it is hard not to have some sympathy with the Court of Appeal's more relaxed approach – at least insofar it extends to commercial parties.

As elsewhere, the balance struck by s 14(2) as to performance risk between buyer and seller is the product of evolution over time. Before the Sale of Goods Act 1893, the courts recognised that a seller could in some circumstances be liable for latent defects even where not part of the description of the goods (Bridge 2019b, 412–13). Sir Mackenzie Chalmers then drafted the 1893 Act to recognise a freestanding implied term for 'merchantable quality' for all sales by description, but he did not attempt to define what 'merchantable' meant, giving rise to a mass of difficult case law. The statute was not amended to include a definition until 1973. That definition focused on whether the goods were fit for the purpose or purposes for which they were commonly bought. That was felt to be little better and so, by the Sale and Supply of Goods Act 1994, the statute switched to a test of 'satisfactory quality' for all sales, defined in s 14(2A) as being what 'a reasonable person would regard as satisfactory' with a whole checklist of factors at s 14(2A)–(2B) to consider beyond description and price (fitness for all common purposes, appearance and finish, minor defects, safety, durability).

The Law Commission project leading to the 1994 amendments (Law Commission 1987) was influenced in its recommendations by the fact that the 1979 Act then applied to consumers as well as commercial parties. But it was obviously wrong for those reforms to seek to prescribe a 'one size fits all' test for the allocation of qualitative performance risk for both commercial and consumer transactions. A desire to protect consumers when buying goods led to an overly generous system for commercial buyers. That unitary approach has now changed with the introduction of the Consumer Rights Act 2015. However, regrettably no amendments have since been made to s 14(2), (2A) and (2B) to move the default allocation risk in commercial transactions back towards something which would be more appropriate. Commercial buyers are still over-protected by the default rule.

By way of example, before the 1973 amendments, the courts had adopted a commercial approach towards merchantable quality by asking whether the goods were fit for at least *one* such purpose: *Henry Kendall & Sons v William Lillico & Sons Ltd* [1969] 2 AC 31. That position remained the case up to the 1994 amendments. As Lloyd LJ said *M/S Aswan Engineering Establishment Co v Lupdine Ltd* [1987] 1 WLR 1, at 12, in order to comply with s 14(2) 'the goods did not have to be suitable for every purpose within a range of purposes for which goods were normally bought under that description. It was sufficient that they were suitable for one or more such purposes'. The Law Commission decided that the law should be changed on this point (Law Commission 1987, 28–29). But it seems wrong that the default setting in the commercial context may be that all goods sold should be fit for *all* purposes for which they are commonly supplied, as is now suggested by s 14(2B)(a). Although s 14(2B) itself says that this is only in 'appropriate cases', which gives the courts some latitude, that flexibility (if it to be used) also engenders a good deal of uncertainty. In any event, if the buyer had a particular purpose in mind which was not that purpose, it should be for the buyer to raise that point with the seller to bargain for an express warranty or to bring it within s 14(3), which is considered next.

(5) *Reasonableness fitness for a communicated purpose.* If a buyer impliedly or expressly communicates to the seller that the goods are for a particular purpose, even if not a common purpose, the qualitative performance risk lies on the seller to ensure that the goods are reasonably fit for that communicated purpose: s 14(3) of the 1979 Act. The risk assumed by the seller is not a strict warranty that the goods will be fit for the stated purpose, but rather that it should be reasonably so. This is capable of covering latent as well as patent defects. However, as Lord Pearce explained in *Kendall v Lillico* (at 115), ultimately this requires weighing 'the rarity of the unsuitability' against 'the gravity of its consequences'. Lord Pearce gave the example of a car. In the English climate, a car which was unpleasant in a heat wave would probably still be reasonably fit for purpose, but not if it was instead ill-suited for rain. But if the car was lethally dangerous in a heat wave, then it would not be reasonably fit for purpose.

The seller can only shift this risk back to the buyer if either he insists on a term in the contract to exclude s 14(3) or if it can be shown that the buyer did not rely on the skill or judgment of the seller or it would have been unreasonable for the buyer to do so. The reliance does not need to be total; it suffices that the matter later complained of fell within the zone of matters where the buyer was relying on the seller. So, for example, in *Cammell Laird & Co Ltd v Manganese Bronze & Brass Co Ltd* [1934] AC 402, the seller was contracted to manufacture two propellers subject to a specified design. The design provided the general dimensions left other matters to the seller's discretion. The seller complied with the design but produced propellers that made too much noise to be used. They were held to be liable because the fault lay not in the design stipulated by the buyer but in those matters left to the seller's skill and judgement.

There is a sliding scale as to the extent to which the purpose has to be made known to the seller before the performance risk is transferred. Sometimes very little needs to be said. If the goods only have one ordinary purpose, the buyer does not really need to say anything more about that particular purpose: *Grant v Australian Knitting Mills Ltd* [1936] AC 85, at 99 (per Lord Wright). Likewise, in *Manchester Liners Ltd v Rea Ltd* [1922] 2 AC 74, a Manchester shipowner ordered coal from Liverpool merchants for their steamship. The coal was suitable for use generally but not suitable for the buyer's steamship; the merchants were held liable because they had been told about the vessel for which coal was going to be used. On the other hand, in *Slater v Finning Ltd* [1997] AC 473 the buyer's fishing vessel experienced repeated mechanical difficulties. The seller sent engineers who advised the buyer to replace the camshaft in their fishing vessel, which was not working well. The replacement camshaft for a fishing vessel worked for other vessels but caused excessive noise and wear on the buyer's ship. The seller was held not to be liable. Lord Keith characterised the fishing vessel as having an 'abnormality' or 'idiosyncrasy' (at 482) which required a special form of camshaft and considered that there could be no liability on the seller where the idiosyncrasy itself had not been communicated to the seller.

It is not clear what separates *Manchester Liners* from *Slater v Finning*. It may be that the coal would have been unsuitable for any steamship of that type, whereas the fishing vessel had developed one-of-a-kind mechanical features rendering the camshaft unsuitable that otherwise would have been suitable for vessels of that type. The Law Lords in *Slater v Finning* did not directly deal with the earlier case but they did place particular weight on a consumer case, *Griffiths v Peter Conway Ltd* [1939] 1 All ER 685, where a consumer bought a coat that was unsuitable for her unusually sensitive skin. In *Griffiths*, Sir Wilfrid Greene MR distinguished *Manchester Liners* (at 692–93) on the basis that the coal merchants were sufficiently specialised to have known what different steamships required whereas Mrs Griffith's skin condition was 'something abnormal, unknown, which no seller could assume to exist'. But in *Slater v Finning* the seller's engineers had worked on the fishing vessel before recommending the camshaft, so it is less easy to say that its special mechanical requirements could simply be treated as unknown (or unknowable).

REMEDIES I: TERMINATION AND REJECTION

If the implied qualitative term breached by the seller is a condition, rather than a warranty, they may be entitled to terminate the contract and reject the goods or services, thereby making a qualitative breach a quantitative breach and opening up the remedies discussed earlier in the chapter (see pages 105–10 above). So, for example, a buyer of goods can avoid suing for damages for late performance or defective goods (if they so wish) by rejecting the goods and then suing for non-delivery or restitution of the purchase price.

This ability to make a qualitative breach a quantitative one can be demonstrated by looking at the framework of the 1979 Act, where terms implied by ss 13, 14 and 15 are conditions. At common law, as codified in s 11, any breach would entitle the seller to terminate or reject. This has been modified by s 15A which waters these conditions down to something closer to innominate terms. Rejection is now prohibited where the breach was so slight that it would be unreasonable to reject the goods. This goes some way to redress the performance risk otherwise placed on the seller before the remedial stage of the analysis.

Termination and rejection are not automatic remedies. The buyer has a choice, or 'election', which arises once the breach has occurred and is known about. In a sales context, the contract will be affirmed and the right of rejection lost when the goods are accepted. This is regulated by ss 34 and 35 which give the buyer a 'reasonable opportunity of examining the goods' after delivery and then deems acceptance in three scenarios: (i) where acceptance is 'intimated', (ii) where the seller then does an act which is inconsistent with the seller's title and (iii) after passage of a reasonable length of time without rejection.

The *first* of these scenarios is relatively straightforward, and nothing more need be said about it. The *second* is more complex. Ordinarily, if the buyer sells on the goods, that is an act inconsistent with the seller's title. But the buyer may enter into a string contract before having an opportunity to examine the goods. The right to such an opportunity is expressed to take priority over the rule deeming acceptance, and s 35(6) provides that the buyer cannot be deemed to have accepted the goods 'merely ... because the goods are delivered to another under a sub-sale or other disposition'. But the 1979 Act does not identify what more is required. Of course, if the goods cannot be returned because (for example) the buyer has no right to recover the goods from the sub-buyer, that would obviously be inconsistent with the seller's title. Otherwise, the best that can be done is to fall back on the overarching question of whether the contract has been affirmed (Goode and McKendrick 2020, 417–18).

As to the *third* scenario, the length of time will depend on the circumstances but is unlikely in most commercial cases to be a particularly lengthy period. Most of the case law concerns consumers. In *Bernstein v Pamson Motors (Golders Green) Ltd* [1987] 2 All ER 200 the car broke down on its first long trip but some three weeks after delivery; that was held too long. In *Jones v Gallagher* [2004] EWCA Civ 10 the defect in a delivered kitchen unit was patent not latent, and so would have been apparent on delivery or soon after in late April. In early May, the buyer wrote to complain about the quality of what had been provided but there was no suggestion that the kitchen should be returned until September. Again, this was too late. The buyer in *Jones* relied on an earlier decision in *Clegg v Andersson* [2003] EWCA Civ 320, a case about the sale of a yacht. There, time was in effect stopped from running for the period that the parties entered into discussions to see if the yacht could be repaired, allowing rejection to take place some six months after delivery. The Court in *Jones* distinguished *Clegg* on the basis that the defects in the earlier case were complex; in the later case the defects were straightforward to communicate and consider for repair purposes.

REMEDIES II: DAMAGES

Damages for qualitative breaches follow the same compensation principle as for quantitative breaches. Again, legal causation and remoteness play important functions in limiting the seller's potential exposure to performance risk.

Many of the leading contract damages cases involve delayed performance. In *Hadley v Baxendale* (1854) 9 Ex 341, the claim concerned the loss caused by the five-day delay in carriage of a broken crankshaft for repair, without which a mill could not operate. The mill owners' claim for five days' lost profits was dismissed as being for too remote a loss; the carriers had no reasonable way of knowing that there was no spare shaft that could be used while the repair was being carried out. On the other hand, in *Victoria Laundry (Windsor) Ltd v Newman Industries Ltd* [1949] 2 KB 528, where a five-month delay in delivering a new boiler caused a laundry business a loss of profits, Asquith LJ held (at 539–40) that it was sufficient at the time of contracting to contemplate as a 'serious possibility' or 'real danger' the business might be without a working boiler, and so the seller was liable for the loss of profit (but only ordinary profits – the loss of one particularly lucrative contract being held to be too remote as it was not in the reasonable contemplation of the parties at the time of contracting).

Both *Hadley v Baxendale* and *Victoria Laundry* concerned transactions where the buyer wanted the relevant item for use in the business. But similar issues arise where the delayed delivery of goods causes the buyer to suffer loss in respect of sub-sales. The main debate is whether to measure loss by reference to market prices in the same way as for damages for non-delivery and non-acceptance discussed at pages 108–10 above.

In *Wertheim v Chicoutimi Pulp Co* [1911] AC 301, a German firm contracted to import wood pulp from Canada. However, the wood pulp was shipped late using, as it happened, the very same steamship at issue in *Manchester Liners*, discussed at page 116 above. The market price for wood pulp between the date agreed for delivery and the date of actual delivery fell but the claimant had not suffered this loss because the claimant had already entered into sub-sales which it performed without any difficulties. The claimant insisted that these sub-sales were to be ignored in preference for an application of a difference in market prices but the Privy Council rejected this, Lord Atkinson saying that that measure 'merely designed' to apply the compensation principle, rather than to override it (at 307).

Bridge suggests, with some force, that the key to *Wertheim*'s reluctance to use a market measure is that the contract was never terminated, so the buyer never needed to go into the market as a matter of mitigation (Bridge 2016b, 415). The oddity in *Wertheim* is that, despite suffering no loss, the claimant was still awarded the difference between the market price on the agreed date for delivery and the sub-sale price. Substitutive damages theorists suggest this was substitute for the infringed right for timely delivery (Stevens 2009, 183–84). The only compensatory explanation is that, if these were string sales (and the law report is not clear on this), this justified looking at the sub-sales in the same way as in *Hall v Pim*, discussed at pages 109–10 above.

In *Koufos v C Czarnikow Ltd (The Heron II)* [1969] 1 AC 350, a claim was made for delivery of sugar to Basra in Iraq, delayed by nine days in breach of charterparty. The price for sugar in those nine days had fallen. The charterer claimed the difference by way of damages. The shipowner was aware of the existence of a sugar market in Basra but did not know that the charterer had intended to sell the sugar promptly in that market upon delivery, and argued that this meant that the market loss was too remote. That argument was rejected by the House of Lords who held that it was sufficient that it was 'not unlikely' (Lord Reid at 383). Although Lord Reid made it clear in *The Heron II* that he disagreed with the substance of the *Victoria Laundry* 'serious possibility' test, he was alone amongst the Law Lords on that point, and more recently the difference between the two has been treated as being merely a disagreement about the 'choice of language': *Attorney General of the Virgin Islands v Global Water Associates Ltd* [2021] AC 23, at [28] (per Lord Hodge).

For a long time, it appeared that a non-compensatory approach was taken for damages for defective goods, at least where intended for re-sale rather than use in the business. Section 53 of the 1979 Act provides for a default measure of the difference between the market value of the goods as delivered and those that ought to have been delivered. This has been argued to represent 'the value of the contractual right at the time of performance (Stevens 2009, 179). So, in *Slater v Hoyle & Smith Ltd* [1920] 2 KB 11 (CA), the buyer sued the seller for supplying inferior cotton but was able to sell on without any reduction in profit. Despite this, the Court held that the buyer could recover the difference in value without any reference to the sub-sales. *Wertheim* was doubted, with the Court preferring to follow the reasoning in *Williams v Agius* (discussed at page 109 above).

The opposite outcome was reached in *Bence Graphics International Ltd v Fasson UK Ltd* [1998] QB 87, where defective vinyl film was bought by the buyer and used to make shipping container labels, but with few complaints being made by end users of the manufactured product. The market rule in section 53 was disapplied and the buyer was limited to any losses suffered on the sub-sales. The Court was clearly uncomfortable with the apparent disjuncture between the compensation principle and the outcome in *Slater*. Otton LJ unconvincingly distinguished *Slater* (at 99) on the basis that it had not involved a manufacturing process (why that mattered was not explained) and because the seller had not known about the contemplated sub-sales (an obvious misapplication of remoteness reasoning). Auld LJ rightly had reservations about these points of distinction and was more transparent about the tension between the cases, criticising *Slater* as having 'too much regard to practicality at the expense of principle' (at 105).

Most commentary has assumed (like Auld LJ) that there is no way of reconciling *Slater* with *Bence Graphics*, and one should be overruled in favour of the other (Bridge 2016b, 417–19; Stevens 2009, 179–80). However, reconciliation is possible on the basis of legal causation or mitigation (Dyson and Kramer 2014, 274–75). The defect in the cotton in *Slater* was *patent* and so the reasonable act of mitigation would have been to go into the market and buy substitute cotton to perform the sub-sales rather than still try to sell the cotton on; the buyer having failed to do that, they were treated as if they had. In contrast, in *Bence*, the defect was *latent* and the breach was discovered only after the sub-sales had been fulfilled. In those circumstances, the buyer had acted reasonably in selling on the defective film, and so, as a matter of legal causation, the lack of actual loss could not be ignored.

6

Credit Risk

This chapter is about credit risk, in the second sense introduced in chapter one. In other words, this chapter is not about the species of performance risk where the party who has rendered goods, services or credit asks whether the counterparty will pay on time or otherwise. Rather, this chapter is about the problems which arise when the issue is whether the counterparty *can* pay and, more to the point, if they cannot, what can be done to mitigate against the effect of the counterparty's insolvency. It is necessary to say something about insolvency law first, before then turning to the techniques for mitigating exposure to this risk.

1. INSOLVENCY

TRANSFER OF RISK FROM INVESTORS TO CREDITORS

Very small commercial enterprises may take sole trader form. If the trader is unable to pay their debts, they may be made bankrupt. In return for their debts being discharged, all the bankrupt's assets – both in the business and personal – will then vest in a 'trustee in bankruptcy' who is tasked to realise the assets, and distribute the proceeds of that estate to creditors (ss 305 and 324 of the Insolvency Act 1986). (In this chapter, references to the 1986 Act are to the Insolvency Act 1986.) The risk of losing everything obviously makes this an unattractive form of doing business. And sole trader status also limits the potential to scale up business. Most commercial enterprises therefore use companies and partnerships as their vehicles for trading. Unlike sole traders, these vehicles hold their own pools of assets distinct from those of their stakeholders.

For the first part of the industrial revolution, the partnership was the principal form of doing business. The Bubble Act 1720 prohibited the formation of new companies without Royal Charter or specific Act of Parliament. There is a debate about whether the 1720 Act was passed to prevent the speculation seen with the South Sea Company or to prevent other companies competing with the South Sea Company for capital. Whatever the reason, after the South Sea Bubble 'popped' later in 1720, the Act was kept in place until 1825 – although it was weakly enforced and often evaded in the meantime.

Partnerships arise where two or more people (that is, the partners) carry on business together with a view to profit. Partnerships were originally creatures of the common law, but the law was partly codified by the Partnership Act 1890. A partnership under the 1890 Act is not its own entity: it contracts in the names of the partners, and partnership property is instead held on trust by the partners. That meant that if partners are made bankrupt, the assets are still segregated for partnership (rather than personal) creditors. On the other hand, partners' liabilities for the debts and obligations of the partnership are unlimited, which makes this still a potentially risky vehicle for doing business.

After 1825, a series of statutes were passed to develop the limited company as an alternative vehicle for commerce. The company as it emerged in the nineteenth century had several advantages, and it rapidly supplanted the partnership as the main vehicle for trading. In particular, the Joint Stock Companies Act 1844 established the company as a separate legal entity. That meant that companies could contract and hold property in their own name, acting via the rules of agency discussed in chapter three. This created a better-defined pool of assets for the business than the use of trusts in partnership law. However, at this stage, shareholders – like partners – remained liable in full for the company's debts.

That changed with the Limited Liability Act 1855, as then consolidated into the Joint Stock Companies Act 1856. Under the 1855–56 Acts, shareholders were not liable for limited company debts beyond the amount required to pay up the shares. In essence this was a *transfer* of credit risk: it reduced the exposure for investors, and correspondingly increased the credit risk for those dealing with companies. The purpose of this reform was to encourage investment in the increasingly large and capital-hungry companies – such as railway companies – then being incorporated. Unlike most early companies, where shareholders were often intimately involved in the running of the company, these larger companies raised large amounts of capital from a wide base of shareholders, most of whom would be passive investors, and so would be reluctant to invest without some limit to their exposure on any failure of the company. The development of partnerships and companies required new rules governing what was to happen when they are unable to pay their debts. These were developed from the law of bankruptcy (although bankruptcy law was itself and in parallel subject to substantial statutory reform from the mid-nineteenth century). Given their greater commercial significance, this chapter focuses on principles of corporate insolvency, that is, the rules governing when companies are unable to pay their debts. But the rules governing the failure of other types of commercial vehicles are not dissimilar.

LIQUIDATION

When a company's liabilities exceed its assets ('balance sheet' insolvency) or the company is unable to pay its debts as they fall due ('cash flow' insolvency) it may put itself into liquidation or be wound up on the petition of a creditor ('liquidation' and 'winding up' are two names for the same process). Liquidation has the same basic idea as bankruptcy: an insolvency officeholder called a 'liquidator' is appointed, tasked to realise the company's assets and distribute the proceeds of that estate to creditors (ss 107 and 143 of the 1986 Act). As a company has its own legal personality, title to the assets does not need to vest in the liquidator; instead, the liquidator takes control of the company itself, authorised by law to act on its behalf instead of the directors (see page 71 above). From the moment that the winding up begins, individual creditor claims are or can be stayed (ss 112 and 130 of the 1986 Act). And once the available assets are all realised and proceeds distributed, the company is dissolved; that is, it ceases to exist. Unlike bankruptcy, however, there is no general discharge or release of debts.

Liquidation is best understood as a procedure – a class remedy or collective enforcement mechanism for creditors – and so the starting point is that it does not disturb *pre*-liquidation personal or proprietary rights and obligations: *Wight v Eckhardt* [2004] 1 AC 147, at [26]–[27] (per Lord Hoffmann). However, this is subject to various statutory exceptions, such as insolvency set-off (see pages 97–98 above), specific powers given to liquidators to claw back assets or disclaim onerous property, and rules dealing with future and contingent debts at the time of liquidation. There is a debate as to whether these exceptions are now so numerous as to call into question the basic procedural premise of liquidation. The Supreme Court divided on this issue in *Re Lehman Bros International (Europe) (No 4)* [2018] AC 465, albeit that the issue did not need finally to be determined. Lord Neuberger was inclined to think of the insolvency process as substantively affecting creditors' pre-insolvency entitlements (at [97]–[111]) whereas Lord Sumption powerfully argued that 'English corporate insolvency law has from its inception adopted the principle … that liquidation was a mode of collective enforcement of debts, which operated procedurally and administratively rather than substantively' (at [195]–[201]).

The procedural view of insolvency law, focused on creditor entitlements, has come under sustained attack from other quarters as well. The 1986 Act was preceded by a landmark report (the 'Cork Report' after its chairman) which noted that 'the effects of insolvency are not limited to the private interests of the insolvent and his creditors, but that other interests of society or other groups in society are vitally affected by the insolvency and its outcome … these public interests [should be] recognised and safeguarded' (Cork 1982, [198]). Academics have similarly argued that insolvency 'encompasses a number of competing – and sometime conflicting – values … no one value dominates, so that bankruptcy policy becomes a composite of factors that bear on a better answer to the question, "How shall the losses be distributed?"' (Warren 1987, 777).

There is considerable force in these points, but they do not require an abandonment of the idea of liquidation as a class remedy for creditors. Instead, they have resulted in a gradual broadening of corporate insolvency law to offer a series of *alternatives* to the creditor-focused liquidation procedure. These alternatives seek to promote a 'rescue culture', recognising that if companies are turned around (even if at a cost to investors and creditors) that is preferable to liquidation from a broader economic and societal perspective. These are considered next.

ADMINSTRATION

The Cork Report's proposed principal alternative to liquidation was administration. This was first introduced by the Insolvency Act 1985, consolidated into the 1986 Act, and then substantially improved by amendments to the 1986 Act introduced by the Enterprise Act 2002. Like liquidation, in administration an insolvency officeholder (an 'administrator') is appointed and authorised to take over from company directors, and the company then enjoys a moratorium that prevents individual creditors from progressing their claims. However, the administrator's duties can differ radically from those of a liquidator. In administration (schedule B1, para 3 of the 1986 Act):

(1) The primary statutory objective is to rescue the company as a going concern.

(2) If that is not reasonably possible, or if it would be better for creditors than rescuing the company, the administrator can fall back on a secondary objective of achieving a better financial return for creditors than had it been put immediately into liquidation.

(3) If that secondary objective is not possible, the administrator must fall back on the third objective of making realisations to distribute to secured or preferential creditors (see further pages 132–33 below).

There are therefore a range of possible outcomes. The company (or its business) may well exit administration and trade as a solvent company again, or it might undergo some other restructuring process (discussed next), or the administration might end up acting as a functional equivalent to a distributing liquidation (leading directly to the dissolution of the company), or the company might be transferred into liquidation (and then on to dissolution).

RESTRUCTURING

As an alternative to an administration – or within it – there are tools by which a majority of creditors can vote to force all creditors (or the relevant group of them) to agree to defer, write-down, swap debt for equity or otherwise restructure their debts so as to allow the company to continue as a going concern. There are now four such mechanisms, none of which entail the company directors surrendering their control to insolvency officeholders (unless the company is also in administration). In brief outline, these are as follows:

(1) *The company voluntary arrangement or 'CVA'*. These require a 75 per cent voting creditor majority in value and bind all creditors eligible to vote, with no requirement also to obtain a sanction from court.

However, CVAs are a relatively weak restructuring tool, most notably being unable to bind non-consenting secured creditors. Given the central position of secured creditors in the balance sheets of most trading companies, this is a severe limitation.

(2) *The scheme of arrangement.* Unlike CVAs, these take place under the supervision of the court. A majority of 75 per cent in value and a majority in number of each relevant class of creditors (that is, creditors whose rights are sufficiently similar so as to have a shared interest in the outcome) must vote for the proposal, and the court also must be persuaded to sanction the scheme as being fair for creditors generally. The advantage of schemes is that they can bind non-consenting secured creditors. However, schemes cannot be sanctioned if the relevant majority thresholds are not met for each class of creditors.

(3) *The restructuring plan.* The Corporate Insolvency and Governance Act 2020 amended the Companies Act 2006 to create a 'cross-class cram down' tool in the form of the restructuring plan. This is a powerful new tool, not only because it does not require a majority of creditors in number to vote as opposed to a majority by value (conferring greater power on larger creditors, such as banks), but more importantly because it enables the plan to be implemented by court order even where a particular creditor class does not reach the 75 per cent threshold. However, this is only available if (i) the company is in financial difficulties threatening its going concern status, (ii) no dissenting creditor class would be worse off under the plan than in the 'relevant alternative' (ie what is likely to happen to the company without a restructuring, such as liquidation or administration) and (iii) the plan has been approved at least by one class of creditors at the 75 per cent threshold who have a legitimate economic interest in its outcome (ie stand to write off some of their debt in return for payment under the plan, or would have an ongoing economic interest in the company in the 'relevant alternative').

(4) *The moratorium.* The 2020 Act also amended the 1986 Act to introduce a stand-alone moratorium procedure, which some companies can enter into for a short period of time to stay creditor claims. The intention of this reform is to give the company breathing space to enter into some other form of corporate rescue or restructuring. Moratoriums can initially be entered into out of court, but the court will become involved to deal with extensions beyond 40 business days.

Where the underlying fundamentals of a company's trade are sound but it is struggling with the debt on its balance sheet, creditors may not need to invoke any of the above legislative options for a majority-dictated restructuring, still less liquidation or administration. Creditors may be able to agree a standstill period between them and then negotiate in a coordinated way with the company to vary its debt obligations. Creditors are incentivised to participate in this process if they think it likely that it will lead to a better return than a more formal insolvency process or restructuring tool.

THE DEFAULT POSITION OF CREDITORS WHERE THERE IS NO RESCUE

Where rescue efforts are not pursued, are not available or fail, the starting point for creditors in liquidations and distributing administrations is that they can participate pro rata in distributions from the estate. Suppose, for example, a liquidator or the administrator realises £1 million in assets and the company owes £10 million: £5 million to the bank, £1 million to each of its four major trade creditors and £100,000 each to 10 minor trade creditors. The proceeds from the company's estate would be distributed as follows: £500,000 to the bank, £100,000 to each major trade creditor and £10,000 to each minor trade creditor. This is known as the *pari passu* principle.

There has been a considerable amount of debate about why this is so. US scholarship has been dominated by arguments for and against the theory of insolvency law as representing a hypothetical bargain between creditors. This posits circumstances where insolvency is a foreseeable risk but has not yet happened, and where creditors are negotiating behind a 'veil of ignorance' that enables them to take a more objective or disinterested approach, without knowing their own individual interest in the insolvency process (see Jackson 1986, 15–17; Jackson and Scott 1989, 160–64). The argument of those in favour of this hypothetical bargain is that a *pari passu* distribution is likely to be what creditors would agree if they did not know their own individual status within the insolvency.

While this argument is theoretically attractive, the notion of the creditors' bargain is not a realistic account of how insolvency law has developed. The reality is that Parliament imposed a *pari passu* principle, and self-interested creditors have – entirely understandably – then sought to find ways to mitigate insolvency risk and create better outcomes for themselves at a cost to other creditors. In response, Parliament and the courts have had to consider to what extent *pari passu* is a mandatory rather than a default rule. The leading case now is *Belmont Park Investments Pty Ltd v BNY Corporate Trustee Services Ltd* [2012] 1 AC 383, where Lord Collins said at [1] that there was a 'general principle that parties cannot contract out of the insolvency legislation'. But it is important not to overstate the strength of the *pari passu* principle. This is seen in the limitations of its two constituent rules.

(1) *The anti-deprivation rule.* The anti-deprivation rule provides that parties cannot transact on the basis that liquidation or administration can act as a trigger to proprietary entitlements that permit the creditor to remove some asset from the estate. But this is a very weak rule after *Belmont,* since it cannot apply to 'bona fide commercial transactions which do not have as their predominant purpose, or one of their main purposes, the deprivation of the property of one of the parties on bankruptcy' (Lord Collins at [104]). In other words, unless there is a deliberate intent to defeat the insolvency regime, the creation of so-called these 'flawed assets' will be valid. And for leases and licences of land, even where there *is* such an intention, the arrangements still will not be impugned. This approach has been rightly criticised as being difficult to apply in practice and 'effectively emasculates' the rule (Worthington 2012, 116–17).

In *Lomas v JFB Firth Rixson Inc* [2012] 2 All ER (Comm) 1076, the ISDA master agreement – the standard terms used for many terms of financial derivatives, such as interest rate swaps – were challenged under the anti-deprivation rule. In an interest rate swap using the ISDA master agreement, party A would pay to party B a sum due by reference to a fixed rate, and receive in return from party B a sum due by reference to a floating rate, with those countervailing payments obligations then being netted into a single sum on each payment date (see pages 96–97 above). But the master agreement provided for the parties' payment obligations to be contingent on no 'event of default', which was defined to include entry into liquidation or administration. So if party B was in liquidation or administration, that condition precedent would not be satisfied, and the payment obligations under the swap by both party A and party B would be suspended.

Like any other debt, this payment obligation can be seen as an asset to be realised in the estate. Administrators challenged the 'event of default' conditionality as infringing the anti-deprivation rule. Applying the emasculated rule in *Belmont,* Longmore LJ dismissed this contention (at [87]–[94]). He considered that the master agreement was formulated to mitigate against credit risk during the life of the contract, in circumstances where one party would want to avoid continuing to fulfil its payment obligations when the counterparty was in administration or liquidation and unlikely to reciprocate. It could not be characterised as a bad faith attempt deliberately to avoid the effect of insolvency law or enhance a return from the insolvent estate (even though that was its effect).

(2) *The pari passu rule.* The *pari passu* rule (distinct from the broader *pari passu* principle) does not attack provisions to remove assets from the estate like the anti-deprivation rule, but rather provides that parties cannot contract for a non pro rata distribution on insolvency. So, to go back to the example at page 129 above, the minor trade creditor cannot agree with the debtor that the debtor will pay £100,000 for goods or services supplied if the debtor is solvent, but £1 million for those goods if the debtor goes into liquidation, thereby artificially enhancing its claim to a share of the liquidation estate.

The reasoning of the majority in *British Eagle International Airlines Ltd v Compagnie Nationale Air France* [1975] 1 All ER 390 is along the same lines, but the facts were more complicated. There, airlines set up a system whereby amounts due to each other under the International Air Transport Association would be netted off each month using contractual set-off (see pages 96–97 above). When British Eagle went into insolvency, the liquidators successful argued that this contravened the *pari passu* rule because it had the effect of giving individual airline creditors of British Eagle a greater distribution than they would be entitled to on a pro rata basis. This was even though there was no suggestion that the netting system was in any way in bad faith; it was as legitimate a mitigation of credit risk as the provisions of the ISDA master agreement arrangements upheld in *Lomas v JFB Firth Rixson*.

In principle, this is a stronger rule than the anti-deprivation rule because it does not turn on whether the parties intended to commit a 'fraud on the statute'. However, it is limited to contractual arrangements; only the anti-deprivation rule can attack proprietary arrangements. The arrangement in *Lomas v JFB Firth Rixson* also survived challenge under the *pari passu* rule, on the basis 'it operates at most to prevent the relevant debt ever becoming payable' (at [98]). The *pari passu* rule also is focused on arrangements by which a creditor seeks to *increase* their share of the insolvency estate; there is no objection to creditors agreeing to *decrease* or 'subordinate' their interests, contracting not to be paid until other creditors have been paid in full: *Re Maxwell Communications Corp (No 2)* [1994] 1 All ER 737.

Neither the anti-deprivation rule nor the *pari passu* rule can invalidate true security arrangements, which provide a proprietary 'hook' for creditors to fish out particular assets from the estate to satisfy their debts in preference to others. The better insolvency outcome for the secured creditor (at a cost to other creditors) is then conditioned by their pre-existing proprietary entitlements. In such a case, the anti-deprivation rule does not apply because security interests are granted *before* insolvency, rather than being triggered *by* insolvency. And the *pari passu* rule does not apply because security interests are proprietary interests rather than operating purely by contract. Parliament could of course intervene to prevent creditors obtaining priority in this way but, as we will see, it has only acted to differentiate between floating charges and other types of security (and to require registration, so that other creditors are on notice) rather than imposing a blanket prohibition on this form of credit risk mitigation.

A further challenge to the strength of the overarching *pari passu* principle is that Parliament *itself* has created multiple exceptions to it. Some of these are market specific, to protect (for example) multilateral netting systems of the type invalidated in *British Eagle* that are seen as systemically important (Part VII of the Companies Act 1989). Other exceptions are more generalised. Insolvency set-off – discussed at pages 97–98 above – is one example. Another exception, at least in functional terms, is the change made to when title passes in unascertained goods (see pages 30–32 above). Further examples of priority access to the realisations of the company estate include the expenses of officeholders and certain creditors seen as more deserving (so-called preferential creditors) for debts such as unpaid taxes as well as employees (up to a limit).

Simplifying somewhat, that leads to the following 'waterfall' down which the proceeds of realisation of the company's assets cascade, until exhausted (*Re Nortel* [2014] AC 209, at [39] (per Lord Neuberger)):

(1) Relevant secured creditors (and functional proprietary equivalents), other than floating charges;
(2) Liquidator or administrator expenses of the insolvency proceedings;
(3) Preferential creditors (eg taxes; wage bills up to a limit);
(4) Relevant floating charge creditors;
(5) Unsecured creditors (subject to the *pari passu* principle);
(6) Interest;

(7)   In the event of a surplus once all creditors have been paid as above, shareholders.

The cumulative effect of stages (1) to (4) of the waterfall – as well as other exceptions to *pari passu* – is such that, generally, unsecured creditors at stage (5) are left with very little, if anything. The prejudice is primarily caused by the ever more sophisticated ways in which credit risk can be mitigated using security and equivalent proprietary techniques. One leading commentator puts it this way, in powerful terms (van Zwieten 2018, 111–12):

> The result of all of these developments has been disastrous for the ordinary unsecured creditor. Every new property right, every added security interest … has eroded his stake in the insolvency process. Add to this the categories of debt still enjoying preferential status and it can readily be seen that the lot of the general body of creditors is a very unhappy one, with the result that they display understandable apathy when it comes to participation in the insolvency process. The *pari passu* rule remains the guiding principle of distribution in English winding-up, but the free assets available to meet ordinary unsecured claims are in the typical case so small that there is little on which the principle can bite.

It is difficult to see what can be done materially to improve the lot of the unsecured creditor for as long as English law cleaves to a procedural view of liquidation and administration by which, subject to exceptions, pre-insolvency personal or proprietary rights and obligations are not disturbed (see pages 125–26 above). And this reality calls into question the strength of the *pari passu* principle. It may be an overstatement still to describe it as 'one of the most fundamental principles of corporate insolvency law' (van Zwieten 2018, 121). It is better characterised as a default position for creditors who can, subject to the anti-deprivation and *pari passu* rules, relatively easily mitigate their credit risk and bargain for a better insolvency outcome (Mokal 2005, 92–132).

2. MITIGATING CREDIT RISK

THE NATURE OF SECURITY

The essential function of security, placed in this context, is to enable a creditor to bargain for a better outcome – often a much better outcome – on the debtor's insolvency than the default *pari passu* position that would apply if the creditor were unsecured. However, in English law, security is defined not by its function but rather by its conceptual nature. There are three key requirements:

(1) *Security rights are property rights.* First, it is not enough for the debtor to promise the creditor that a particular asset will be used to pay the debt or not used for any other purpose. The asset must be appropriated to the debt, meaning that the creditor has a direct proprietary right in respect of that asset. So, for example, in *Palmer v Carey* [1926] AC 703, an importer borrowed to buy goods for his business. He promised the lender that the proceeds from the domestic sale of the goods imported would be paid into the lender's bank account, who could then deduct whatever was then owed and then pay on the balance to the importer. The Privy Council held there was nothing in that arrangement that gave the lender a proprietary interest in the proceeds. The same conclusion was reached in *Swiss Bank Corp Ltd v Lloyds Bank Ltd* [1982] AC 584, where a borrower promised not to use assets for any more other than to repay the lender. The House of Lords held that this was nothing more than a negative covenant. This proprietary requirement therefore excludes guarantees and flawed asset arrangements from the definition of security, despite their functional equivalence; neither involves the creditor holding proprietary rights.

(2) *Security rights cannot be retained by the creditor.* This second requirement is a reason why RoT arrangements discussed at page 25 above are not considered security under English law: *Armour v Thyssen Edelstahlwerke AG* [1991] 2 AC 339. Although the creditor under a RoT arrangement has a proprietary interest, that is because they have bargained that title will not pass until the sums due have been paid, rather than because the debtor has granted the creditor any such right. In contrast, the definition of security requires the debtor to grant the creditor a fresh proprietary interest in the asset. However, this requirement by itself would not necessarily exclude trusts – such as *Quistclose* trusts (see page 144 below) – from the definition of security. That is because it is not possible for the legal owner of property, when transferring title, to 'retain' an equitable interest. The trust can only arise once there is a separation of legal ownership from beneficial entitlement to property: *Westdeutsche Landesbank Girozentrale v Islington London Borough Council* [1996] AC 669, 706–07 (per Lord Browne-Wilkinson). As trusts are obviously

not security interests, this second requirement is not sufficient to characterise a proprietary arrangement as involving security rights.

(3) *Security rights are limited rights.* This third requirement, then, goes to the essence of the conceptual nature of security. The distinguishing feature of a security right is that it is inherently limited: it is a secondary proprietary right to appropriate the value of the asset up to the value of the primary debt obligation. As Romer LJ explained in *Re George Inglefield Ltd* [1933] Ch 1, at 27–28, this means that, if the primary sum is repaid, the security interest falls away; if the creditor enforces the security and there is still a shortfall, the creditor can still sue for the balance of the primary sum; and, if the creditor enforces the security and there is a surplus after repayment of the primary sum, the creditor must hand the surplus over to debtor (subject to foreclosure: see page 137 below). This requirement excludes both RoT arrangements and trusts from the definition of security. In both cases, the creditor has a beneficial interest (either in law or equity) which goes beyond the value of the primary debt. So, for example, if the buyer of goods under RoT arrangements never pays for them, the seller simply takes the goods back (by virtue of title) and will take any surplus when selling them on to a third party (if the value of the goods have gone up) or suffers the shortfall (if the value of the goods has gone down).

There is a closed list of proprietary interests which meet the requirements set out in the last section. These can be sub-divided into possessory security – pledges and liens – where the creditor must have possession of the asset, and non-possessory security – mortgages and charges – where the debtor can keep possession. An alternative approach is to divide security between those created by way of transfer, and those created by way of agreement alone (Stevens 2011).

Commercial parties cannot create new forms of security. The court's task in a dispute between creditor and debtor (or the debtor's insolvency officeholders) as to the nature of the creditor's entitlements is to (i) construe the rights and obligations created by arrangements and (ii) then seek to place them within one of the existing categories: *Agnew v Commissioner of Inland Revenue* [2001] 2 AC 710, at [32] (per Lord Millett). This is an exercise which looks at substance rather than form; so the fact that the parties have called the arrangements by one label does not preclude the court from reaching a different conclusion. Typically, the dispute will be whether the arrangements are security at all (as opposed to some functional equivalent, such as RoT) or, if security, whether it should be treated as a floating charge such that the creditor is pushed several rungs down the insolvency waterfall set out at pages 132–33 above.

TRANSFER-BASED SECURITY INTERESTS

There are three transfer-based security interests. A *lien* is a right to detain the debtor's choses in possession until money owed has been paid. The creditor will have been delivered possession of the chattels for some purpose *other* than security, but the parties will either have agreed a right of detention when a debt is unpaid or, in certain well-defined circumstances, such a right can arise by operation of law. For example, an unpaid seller of goods can, if still in possession, exercise a lien if not paid when no credit was extended, or the term of credit has expired, or where the buyer becomes insolvent: s 41 of the Sale of Goods Act 1979. Similar detention rights arise by operation of law for the benefit of, for example, repairers, professional advisers and innkeepers. However, the creditor can only go further than detention of the property, and sell it and appropriate the proceeds towards the unpaid debt, if that has been agreed or if there is statutory provision (such as s 48 of the Sale of Goods Act 1979 and ss 12 and 13 of the Torts (Interference with Goods) Act 1977).

The principal difference between a lien and a *pledge* is that, whereas for a lien the creditor has possession of the choses in possession for some reason other than security, for a pledge the creditor is given possession by the debtor with the intention that it should stand as security. Because the property has been delivered for that purpose, the creditor has the right to sell and appropriate the proceeds towards the unpaid debt from the outset, without the need for further agreement or statutory provision. Actual possession is not necessary; it suffices for the creditor to have constructive possession rather than actual possession, such as by the debtor delivering a document of title (for example, a bill of lading) or through attornment (see page 23 above). But there must still be delivery in the sense discussed at page 22 above; that is, a conferral of control over the goods. In *Dublin City Distillery Ltd v Doherty* [1914] AC 823, the distillery offered a lender pledge over whiskey casks by delivering the lender the key to the premises. But two keys were required to access the casks, with the other being held at all times by the tax authorities.

In those circumstances, there was no valid pledge. Lord Atkinson emphasised (at 843): 'a contract to pledge a specific chattel, even though money be advanced on the faith of it, is not in itself sufficient ... Delivery is, in addition, absolutely necessary to complete the pledge'.

A *mortgage* in law or in equity involves a transfer not of possession but of existing title (so-called mortgages in equity which do not take place by way of transfer are better characterised as charges). As a result, a mortgage can in principle be taken not only of land (although by statute this now takes effect by way of charge) and choses in possession but also of choses in action. Although title is passed, a mortgage is still a limited interest because the transfer is subject to an 'equity of redemption', by which the property will be transferred back to the debtor on discharge of the primary debt. On the other hand, a mortgage can be enforced through 'foreclosure' which extinguishes the equity of redemption and makes the creditor the absolute owner, allowing them to keep any surplus but suffer any shortfall. In this sense, a mortgage is a less limited proprietary interest than other forms of security.

AGREEMENT-BASED SECURITY INTERESTS

In contrast with the first three forms of security above, a charge is an agreement-based security interest. It does not involve any delivery of possession, or transfer of existing title, but rather the creation by agreement of a new equitable interest to the property, different from the creation of an express trust only in that the interest is a limited form of proprietary right. As with an express trust, no set recitation of words is required to create a charge; but the parties must objectively intend that the creditor will have a proprietary right against the secured asset that can be realised and applied in discharge of the debt that has been advanced: *National Provincial and Union Bank of England v Charnley* [1924] 1 KB 431, 440 (per Bankes LJ).

The charge has considerable advantages as a technique for mitigating credit risk compared to transfer-based forms of security. Unlike liens and pledges, charges can be created over all forms of property. It can be easier to create a charge than a mortgage, given the requirements to transfer title for mortgage purposes can vary depending on asset class. The courts have been willing to give effect to charges even in the face of conceptual difficulties. So, for example, in *Re Bank of Credit and Commerce International SA (No 8)* [1998] AC 214, the question was whether a bank could take a charge over its customer's account balances. The argument against this was that, as between bank and customer, the bank account represented a personal claim not an asset capable of being used as security (Goode 1998; see also pages 2–3 above). In *obiter dicta*, Lord Hoffmann was not persuaded, saying 'I think that the courts should be very slow to declare a practice of the commercial community to be conceptually impossible' (at 228). Yet it is difficult to see how such a 'charge back' can be enforced other than through set-off, which might be thought to underline the non-proprietary nature of the bank's interest.

A further advantage of the charge is that it can used to take effective security over future assets. In *Holroyd v Marshall* (1862) 10 HL Cas 191, a Yorkshire mill owner in financial distress borrowed £5,000 to avoid the mill's machinery being sold. Security was executed over the existing machinery. The security instrument also provided that any future machinery in the mill would be subject to the same arrangements. The question was whether that security could take effect automatically or would be defeated by the mill owner failing to execute fresh security when acquiring the new machinery. Lord Westbury LC considered that security could arise automatically by applying 'a few elementary principles long settled in Courts of Equity' (at 209). In particular, subject to meeting the Certainties discussed in chapter two (see page 22 above), it sufficed that the parties had agreed the security over future assets in a contract under which valuable consideration had been provided; in those circumstance, the debtor was a 'trustee' of the property in equity pending taking any steps to formalise the security (such as through a conveyance to create a mortgage).

In *Holroyd v Marshall*, Lord Westbury particularly relied on principles of specific performance. This was a circular point: specific performance is available because of the underlying equitable proprietary rights; the availability of specific performance does not determine when such rights arise. The further problem with Lord Westbury's reasoning was that it suggested that charges could only be executed over certain categories of asset (unique assets such as land). In *Tailby v Official Receiver* (1888) 13 App Cas 523, Lord Watson delicately suggested (at 535) that Lord Westbury's reference to specific performance was 'an illustration not selected with his usual felicity' and should be discarded. In that case, a charge was held to take effect over future choses in action in the same way as future choses in possession. In that case, a manufacturer created security over 'all book debts due and owing or which may during the continuance of this security become due and owing'.

The House of Lords recognised that in some cases the Certainties – and, in particular, Subject Matter Certainty – would not be satisfied. But where the Certainties were satisfied, subject to valuable consideration having been given, there was no reason for the book debts to be assigned in equity as part of the security arrangements as soon as they came into existence.

There has been some debate as to what happens if there is a supervening event, such as liquidation, between the creation of a charge over future property and the coming into existence of the property to be charged. In *Re Lind* [1915] 2 Ch 345, the Court of Appeal held that the charge took proprietary effect before the property came into existence, and even where the debtor's bankruptcy occurred before the property came into existence. But an earlier Court of Appeal, led by Sir George Jessel MR, held in *Collyer v Isaacs* (1881) 19 Ch D 342 at 351 that 'until the property comes into existence the contract remains only a contract', and so was released by the bankruptcy. In policy terms, *Collyer* may be seen as preferable as it ensures that a greater share of any insolvent estate is available for *pari passu* distribution. As a matter of precedent, however, it has been recognised that *Re Lind* is the better authority and should be followed: *Peer International Corp v Termidor Music Publishers* [2002] EWHC 2675 (Ch) at [79] (per Neuberger J). *Re Lind* also contains the more persuasive reasoning, recognising that there is no good reason not to give proprietary effect to charges over future property given the validity of express trusts over future property. As Bankes LJ put it (at 374): 'It is true that the security was not enforceable until the property came into existence, but nevertheless the security was there, the assignor was the bare trustee of the assignee to receive and hold the property for him when it came into existence'.

That debate aside, after *Holroyd v Marshall* and *Tailby v Official Receiver*, it was open to lenders to negotiate security over the whole of a debtor's assets present and future, without being encumbered by having to take delivery or a transfer of title. But the debtors (understandably) would want to be able to sell their assets, unless and until any default. As an agreement-based security interest, there was no reason in principle why this could not be done. Victorian lawyers thus negotiated charges over the whole of a company's 'undertaking' (or equivalent) whilst agreeing terms that the company was not restricted from dealing with those assets in the ordinary course of business before any default, but on default such dealings would no longer be permitted and the charge would 'crystallise' (Nolan 2004, 120–24). In *Re Panama, New Zealand and Australian Royal*

Mail Co (1869–70) LR 5 Ch App 318, the Court confirmed the validity of these charges, Giffard LJ saying (at 322) 'I see no difficulty or inconvenience in giving that effect to this instrument'.

FIXED AND FLOATING CHARGES

Giffard LJ did not appear to consider the charge that he upheld in *Re Panama* to be conceptually different from any earlier charge, and that was probably the same understanding as those entrepreneurial lawyers who had developed it: different in scope but not in nature. However, it rapidly become known in practice as a 'floating charge' (Nolan 2004, 122) in contrast to 'fixed' charges that did not permit dealing with the charged assets.

It soon became necessary to draw a firmer distinction between fixed and floating charges. That is because Parliament legislated to make floating charges, as created, less effective, including by pushing them down to a lower rung in the insolvency waterfall than other secured creditors (see page 132 above): ss 40, 175, 176A, 176ZA and 245 and schedule B1, paras 65, 70 and 99 of the 1986 Act. This intervention was necessary because the floating charge would otherwise give too many advantages to a single creditor at the expense of all others. As Lord Millett explained in *Agnew v Commissioner of Inland Revenue* [2001] 2 AC 710, at [9]: 'it enabled the holder of the charge to withdraw all or most of the assets of an insolvent company from the scope of a liquidation and leave the liquidator with little more than an empty shell'. Or, as put memorably by Lord Walker in *Re Spectrum Plus Ltd* [2005] 2 AC 680 at [130] the 'floating charge had become a cuckoo in the nest of corporate insolvency'.

In *Re Yorkshire Woolcombers Association Ltd* [1903] 2 Ch 284 (CA) 295, Romer LJ gave the following famous definition of a floating charge:

> If a charge has the three characteristics that I am about to mention it is a floating charge. (1) If it is a charge on a class of assets of a company present and future; (2) if that class is one which, in the ordinary course of the business of the company, would be changing from time to time; and (3) if you find that by the charge it is contemplated that, until some future step is taken by or on behalf of those interested in the charge, the company may carry on its business in the ordinary way as far as concerns the particular class of assets I am dealing with.

In *Agnew* at [13] and [20], Lord Millett cited this passage approvingly but added that the third characteristic was:

> the hallmark of a floating charge and serves to distinguish it from a fixed charge … the only intention which is relevant is the intention that the company should be free to deal with the charged assets and withdraw them from the security without the consent of the holder of the charge.

Lord Millett's approach was – unsurprisingly – then approved by the House of Lords in *Spectrum* at [107] and [112] (per Lord Scott) and [138]–[139] (per Lord Walker). Thus, after *Agnew* and *Spectrum*:

> [the] essential difference between a fixed and a floating charge turns on the ability of the charger to deal with the charged assets, removing them from the ambit of the security without the consent of the chargee. This, and this alone, provides the characterization test (Worthington 2006, 28).

What remains unclear is whether a fixed charge will become floating if the chargee fetters their ability to refuse consent. A security instrument which stated that the chargee must consent to the withdrawal of assets by the chargor would lead to the charge being characterised as floating. But it is not yet clear what the position would be if the security instrument stated that the chargee should not refuse consent unreasonably, or where consent is deemed unless an objection to dealing is communicated after notice is given.

The litigation in *Agnew* and *Spectrum* itself arose in respect of security over book debts. Floating charges have been capable, from the earliest cases, of applying to receivables. In contrast, the ability to create fixed charges over receivables was not recognised until *Siebe Gorman & Co Ltd v Barclays Bank Ltd* [1979] 2 Lloyd's Rep 142. Although the basis on which Slade J considered a fixed charge arose in that case was later overruled in *Spectrum*, it remains good law that a fixed charge can be created over receivables; the difficult question is when this will be so.

It is now clear, after *Agnew* and *Spectrum*, that fixed charge will not be created over receivables where the debenture provides for payment of all proceeds into an account but there are no express restrictions on the chargee withdrawing from that account (the debenture in *Siebe Gorman*). Nor is there any fixed charge where the parties purport to create a fixed charge over receivables but a floating charge over proceeds (the position taken in *Re New Bullas Trading Ltd* [1994] 1 BCLC 485, but overruled by *Agnew* and *Spectrum*) because receivables and their proceeds cannot

Credit Risk

be treated as separately charged assets: they are two aspects of the same asset.

Put another way, the level of control required for a fixed charge must exist in respect of both the receivables and their proceeds. Sufficient control in that regard can probably be achieved in only a limited number of ways: (i) the chargor could be prohibited from dealing with the proceeds altogether; (ii) the chargor could be permitted only to collect the proceeds and apply them in reduction of the debt owed to the chargee; (iii) the chargor could be authorised as agent to collect the proceeds for the chargee, with those proceeds then held on trust for the chargee; or (iv) the chargor could be permitted to collect the proceeds and pay them into a blocked account with the chargee bank or a third-party bank.

A blocked account arrangement successfully created a fixed charge over receivables in *Re Keenan Bros Ltd* [1986] BCLC 242. The security agreement in that case required the company to pay all monies into a designated bank account and could not be withdrawn from that account without the prior consent of the bank in writing. The Irish Supreme Court held that this sufficed to create a fixed charge. Similarly, in *Re Harmony Care Homes Ltd* [2009] EWHC 1961 (Ch), a charge over receivables was held to be fixed not floating through the use of a blocked account. The chargee had no right of withdrawal: it was not free to deal with the realisation of the receivables or remove them from the account without the chargor's consent. In contrast, in *Gray v G-T-P Group Ltd* [2010] EWHC 1772 (Ch), the charge was characterised as floating in circumstances where, although the chargee had factual control over the proceeds (through payment into a stipulated account), the chargee was required under the security agreement to pay those proceeds onto the chargor upon request at any time before crystallisation of the charge on a default.

JURIDICAL NATURE OF FLOATING CHARGES

Although – as discussed at pages 139–40 above – initially no conceptual distinction was drawn between fixed and floating charges, this rapidly became controversial and conflicting views were taken – sometimes even by the same person. So, for example, in *Governments Stock and Other Securities Investment Co Ltd v Manila Railway Co Ltd* [1897] AC 81, Lord Macnaghten said (at 86) that 'floating security ... attaches to the subject charged in the varying condition in which it happens to be from time to time'. But by *Illingworth v Houldsworth* [1904] AC 355, Lord Macnaghten described (at 358) the security in fundamentally different terms:

> a floating charge … is ambulatory and shifting in its nature, hovering over and so to speak floating with the property which it is intended to affect until some event occurs or some act is done which causes it to settle and fasten on the subject of the charge within its reach and grasp.

There are five main theories in the modern literature as to the juridical nature of floating charges before crystallisation, but all of them have difficulties:

(1) The first theory contends that a floating charge does not confer any proprietary interest at all, until it crystallises into a fixed charge on default (Gough 1996). This would have major implications if it were correct. Often the default under a security instrument is the debtor's entry into liquidation of administration, so if this were the trigger, floating charges would be vulnerable to attack under the anti-deprivation rule. But in fact it is wrong: it is well-established that charge holders have proprietary rights before crystallisation. For example, the permission given to chargees to deal with assets is typically limited to dealings in the ordinary course of business; if there are dealings beyond the ordinary course, the chargee would be entitled to follow or trace and recover those assets.

(2) The second theory is that a floating charge is a fixed charge coupled with a licence to deal or, put another way, a 'defeasible' fixed charge (Worthington 1996, 74–77). This is consistent with the way that floating charges developed out of fixed charges. But it does not explain why a later fixed charge has priority over floating charge at common law; if they were juridically the same type of property right, one would expect the 'first in time' rule to apply. And this theory was also rejected in terms by the Court of Appeal in *Evans v Rival Granite Ltd* [1910] 2 KB 979, where a judgment debt was executed against charge property before crystallisation.

(3) A third theory is the idea that the charge is 'overreached' when assets are dealt with in the ordinary course of business before crystallisation (Nolan 2004, 128–30). The difference between this and the second theory may be one of emphasis: defeasance 'brings an interest to an end' whereas a 'floating charge is an interest that is limited *ab initio* by the mere existence of the chargor's rights to deal with the charged assets free of the

charge'. But even with different language, this theory runs into the same problems as identified at (2) above.

(4) The fourth theory takes seriously Lord Macnaghten's formulation in *Illingworth*, and contends that the floating charge is an immediate but unattached security interest (Gullifer 2022, [4–04]). This was endorsed in *Spectrum* by Lord Walker at [139] but nonetheless is conceptually problematic. There is no such thing as an equitable interest in a fund. At any given time, the interest will be in the property currently making up that fund (Nolan 2004).

(5) The final, and most persuasive, theory is that the floating charge is an equitable power, analogous to the mere equity which exists prior to a right of rescission: just as when the right to rescind is exercised, the mere equity becomes a trust, so too the mere equity represented by the floating charge when crystallised becomes a fixed charge (Stevens 2011, 222–23). This explains why the floating charge is a proprietary interest from the outset, and yet weaker in effect than a fixed charge prior to crystallisation.

OTHER TECHNIQUES FOR MITIGATING CREDIT RISK

Commercial parties are not limited to using security to mitigate exposure to credit risk. We noted at pages 42–43 above that guarantees, insurance, derivatives and letters of credits (adapted into performance bonds) can all be used to protect against the risk of credit defaults. These transfer credit risk from the creditor to a third party, meaning that if the debtor goes insolvent the creditor can look to the solvent third party – such as a parent company or director guarantor, or an insurer, or a credit default swap provider – to make payment instead of the principal debtor.

Set-off, netting and other contractual techniques can also be used to create 'flawed asset' or other contractual structures, which enable creditors to limit their exposure to credit risk. We saw an example of this at pages 130–31 above, where payment obligations under the ISDA master agreement were contingent on each party not being in liquidation or administration were upheld as valid credit risk mitigation arrangements. More generally, well advised commercial actors are able to draft around the weakened anti-deprivation and *pari passu* rules, which are unlikely to invalidate conditional obligations in parties' bargains (Gullifer 2017).

Finally, when supplying goods or capital, commercial parties can negotiate RoT or equivalent provisions. For goods, as we saw at page 25 above, RoT is made possible by ss 17 and 19 of the Sale of Goods Act 1979: nowadays most commercial sellers deal on RoT terms so that, if the buyer goes insolvent, the seller can simply retrieve the goods rather than being limited to proving as an unsecured creditor in the liquidation or administration. The equivalent technique for lenders is to create a *Quistclose* trust, named after *Barclays Bank Ltd v Quistclose Investments Ltd* [1970] AC 567, where money is lent for a stated purpose. This is now best understood, after Lord Millett's judgment in *Twinsectra Ltd v Yardley* [2002] 2 AC 164, to take effect as a resulting trust (arising from a failed express trust) subject to a power to apply the trust monies in accordance with the stated purpose. This protects the lender from the risk of the borrower's insolvency, to the extent that the capital is not applied or misapplied, and bears obvious conceptual similarities to the defeasible or overreaching explanations for floating charges.

ACKNOWLEDGEMENTS

This book owes a great deal to those I have been taught by, and I have taught with, at Cambridge (in no particular order): Louise Gullifer, Louise Merrett, Nick McBride, Jonathan Morgan, Janet O'Sullivan, Julius Grower, Paul Davies, Sarah Worthington and Graham Virgo. Additional thanks go to Nick as a very supportive (and patient!) series editor. A good deal of my thinking has also been shaped by my experience in practice, and the themes which have run through the cases which have come across my desk and which I have argued in court. I am lucky to work with a superb set of colleagues at 3 Verulam Buildings who have helped me along the way with much of the thinking that underpins this book. My thanks also must go to Tham Chee Ho, Rachel Leow and Peter Watts who commented on drafts. I am very grateful to Mr Justice Foxton for his generous foreword. Finally, this book could not have been written without unwavering support and forbearance from my family and particularly my wife, to whom this is dedicated.

BIBLIOGRAPHY

American Law Institute (2006) *Restatement Third, Agency* (American Law Institute Publishers)

Ames, JB (1909) 'Undisclosed Principal – His Rights and Liabilities' 18 *Yale Law Journal* 443

Bailey, SJ (1931) 'Assignments of Debts in England from the Twelfth to the Twentieth Century' 47 *Law Quarterly Review* 516

Barnett, RE (1987) 'Undisclosed Agency Law with Contract Theory' 75 *California Law Review* 1969

Beale, H (2020) 'The New Override of Bans on Assignment of Receivables' in PS Davies and M Raczynska (eds), *Contents of Commercial Contracts: Terms Affecting Freedoms* (Hart Publishing)

Beale, H, Gullifer, L and Paterson, S (2016) 'A Case for Interfering with Freedom of Contract? An Empirically-Informed Study of Bans on Assignment' *Journal of Business Law* 203

Benjamin, J (2007) *Financial Law* (Oxford University Press)

Birks, P (2005) *Unjust Enrichment* 2nd edn (Clarendon Press)

Bridge, MG (2016a) 'The Nature of Assignment and Non-Assignment Clauses' 132 *Law Quarterly Review* 47

—— (2016b) 'Markets and Damages in Sale of Goods Cases' 132 *Law Quarterly Review* 405

—— (2019a) 'Risk, Property and Bulk in International Sales' *Lloyd's Maritime and Commercial Law Quarterly* 57

—— (2019b) *The Sale of Goods* 4th edn (Oxford University Press)

Burrows, A (2012) *The Law of Restitution* 3rd edn (Oxford University Press)

—— (2019) 'In Defence of Unjust Enrichment' 78 *Cambridge Law Journal* 521

Chalmers, M (1890) *The Sale of Goods including the Factors Act 1889* (William Clowes & Sons)

Coke, E (1628) *The First Part of the Institutes of the Lawes of England or a Commentarie upon Littleton* (Society of Stationers)

Conant, M (1968) 'The Objective Theory of Agency: Apparent Authority and the Estoppel of Apparent Ownership' 47 *Nebraska Law Review* 678

Cork, K, and the Review Committee on Insolvency Law and Practice (1982) *Insolvency Law and Practice* (HMSO)

Davies, PS (2020) 'Agency and Rectification' 136 *Law Quarterly Review* 77

Day, W (2016) 'Against Necessity as a Ground for Restitution' *Restitution Law Review* 27

—— (2022) 'Justifications for and Limitations on Interventions by Undisclosed Principals' in PS Davies and Tan CH (eds), *Intermediaries in Commercial Law* (Hart Publishing)

—— (2023) 'Shades of Frustration' in R Probert and E Peel (eds), *Shaping the Law of Obligations: Essays in Honour of Professor Ewan McKendrick* (Oxford University Press)

De Lacy, N (1999) 'The Priority Rule of *Dearle v Hall* Restated' *Conveyancer* 311

Department for Business, Innovation and Skills (2014) *Small Business, Enterprise and Employment Bill: Nullification of Ban on Invoice Assignment Clauses* (BIS/14/1232)

Dowrick, FE (1954) 'The Relationship of Principal and Agent' 17 *Modern Law Review* 24

Dyson, A and Kramer, A (2014) 'There Is No "Breach Date Rule": Mitigation, Difference in Value and Date of Assessment' 130 *Law Quarterly Review* 259

Edelman, J and Elliott, S (2015) 'Two Conceptions of Equitable Assignment' 131 *Law Quarterly Review* 228

Edelman, J, Varuhas, J and Colton, S (2020) *McGregor on Damages* 21st edn (Sweet & Maxwell)

Enonchong, N (2011) *The Independence Principle of Letters of Credits and Demand Guarantees* (Oxford University Press)

Fridman, GHL (2016) 'Undisclosed Principals and the Sale of Goods' in D Busch, L Macgregor and P Watts (eds), *Agency Law in Commercial Practice* (Oxford University Press)

—— (2017) *Canadian Agency Law* 3rd edn (LexisNexis)

Fuller, LL (1941) 'Consideration and Form' 41 *Columbia Law Review* 799

Fox, D (1996) 'The Transfer of Legal Title to Money' *Restitution Law Review* 60

—— (2006) 'Relativity of Title at Law and in Equity' 65 *Cambridge Law Journal* 330

Giliker, P (2010) *Vicarious Liability in Tort: A Comparative Perspective* (Cambridge University Press)

Goff, R (1984) 'Commercial Contracts and the Commercial Court' *Lloyd's Maritime and Commercial Law Quarterly* 382

Goode, R (1998) 'Charge Backs and Legal Fictions' 114 *Law Quarterly Review* 178

—— (2009) 'Contractual Prohibitions against Assignment' *Lloyd's Maritime and Commercial Law Quarterly* 300

Goode, R, and McKendrick, E (2020) *Goode & McKendrick on Commercial Law* (LexisNexis Butterworths)

Goodhart, AL and Hamson, CJ (1932) 'Undisclosed Principals in Contract' 4 *Cambridge Law Journal* 320

Gough, WJ (1996) *Company Charges* 2nd edn (1996)

Gray, K (1991) 'Property in Thin Air' 50 *Cambridge Law Journal* 252

Gullifer, L (2017) 'Flawed Asset Clauses' in G Virgo and S Worthington (eds), *Commercial Remedies: Resolving Controversies* (Cambridge University Press)

—— (2021) 'Property Aspects of Sale of Goods: Interests in Bulk Goods' in M Bridge et al (eds), *The Law of Personal Property* 3rd edn (Sweet & Maxwell)

—— (2022) *Goode and Gullifer on Legal Problems in Credit and Security* 7th edn (Sweet & Maxwell)

Hedley, S (2001) 'Quality of Goods, Information, and the Death of Contract' *Journal of Business Law* 114

Higgins, PFP (1965) 'The Equity of the Undisclosed Principal' 28 *Modern Law Review* 167

Hoffmann, L (1997) 'The Intolerable Wrestle with Words and Meaning' 56 *South African Law Journal* 565

Hohfeld, WN (1917) 'Fundamental Legal Conceptions as Applied in Judicial Reasoning' 26 *The Yale Law Journal* 710

Holdsworth, WS (1920), 'The History of the Treatment of Choses in Action by the Common Law' 33 *Harvard Law Review* 997

Holmes Jnr, OW (1890–91) 'Agency I' 4 *Harvard Law Review* 345

—— (1891–92) 'Agency II' 5 *Harvard Law Review* 1

Honoré, AM (1961) 'Ownership' in AG Guest (ed), *Oxford Essays in Jurisprudence* (Oxford University Press)

Ibbetson, D (1999) *A Historical Introduction to the Law of Obligations* (Oxford University Press)

Jackson, T (1986) *The Logic and Limits of Bankruptcy Law* (Harvard University Press)

Jackson, T, and Scott, RE (1989) 'On the Nature of Bankruptcy: An Essay on Bankruptcy Sharing and the Creditors' Bargain' 75 *Virginia Law Review* 155

Jones, N (2019) 'Henry Sherfield's Reading on Wills (1624) and Trusts in the Form of a Use upon a Use' in D Ibbetson, N Jones and N Ramsay (eds), *English Legal History and its Sources: Essays in honour of John Baker* (Cambridge University Press)

Kramer, A (2005) 'An Agreement-Centred Approach to Remoteness and Contract Damages' in N Cohen and E McKendrick (eds), *Comparative Remedies for Breach of Contract* (Hart Publishing)

Krebs, T (2010) 'Agency Law for Muggles: Why There is No Magic in Agency' in A Burrows and E Peel (eds), *Contract Formation and Parties* (Oxford University Press)

Law Commission (1987) *Sale and Supply of Goods:aw Com No 160* (HMSO)

—— (1993) *Sale of Goods forming Part of a Bulk: Law Com No 215* (HMSO)

Leow, R (2019) 'Understanding Agency: A Proxy Power Definition' 78 *Cambridge Law Journal* 99

Llewellyn, KN (1938) 'Through Title to Contract and a Bit Beyond' 15 *New York University Law Quarterly Review* 159

MacMahon, P (2020) 'Rethinking Assignability' 79 *Cambridge Law Journal* 268

Maitland, FW (1936) *Equity: A Course of Lectures* 2nd edn (Cambridge University Press) Lectures IX–XI.

Mann, FA (1992) *Legal Aspect of Money* 5th edn (Clarendon Press)

McFarlane, B and Stevens, R (2010) 'The Nature of Equitable Property' 4 *Journal of Equity* 1

Merrett, L (2008) 'The Importance of Delivery and Possession in the Passing of Title' 67 *Cambridge Law Journal* 376

Mitchell, C (2020) 'Mercantile Usage, Construction of Contracts and the Implication of Terms, 1750–1850' in C Mitchell and S Watterson (eds), *The World of Maritime and Commercial Law: Essays in Honour of Francis Rose* (Hart Publishing)

Mokal, JM (2005) *Corporate Insolvency Law: Theory and Application* (Oxford University Press)

Morgan, J (2018) 'Common Mistake in Contract: Rare Success and Common Misapprehensions' 77 *Cambridge Law Journal* 559

Müller-Freinfels, W (1953) 'The Undisclosed Principal' 16 *Modern Law Review* 299

Munday, R (1977) 'A Legal History of the Factor' (1977) 6 *Anglo-American Law Review* 221

Nolan, R (2004) 'Property in a Fund' 120 *Law Quarterly Review* 108

O'Meara, BE (1822) *Napoleon In Exile* vol 2 (Simpkin & Marshall)

Oditah, F (1989) 'Equitable versus Legal Assignment of Book Debts' 9 *Oxford Journal of Legal Studies* 513

Pollock, F (1887) 'Notes' 11 *Law Quarterly Review* 355

Pollock, F and Wright, RS (1888) *An Essay on Possession in the Common Law* (Clarendon Press)

Reid, KGC (1997) 'Obligations and Property: Exploring the Border' *Acta Juridica* 225

Reynolds, F (2012) 'Breach of Warranty of Authority in Modern Times' *Lloyd's Maritime and Commercial Law Quarterly* 189

Salmond, J (1907) *Law of Torts* (Stevens & Haynes)

Seavey, WA (1920) 'The Rationale of Agency' 29 *The Yale Law Journal* 859

Smith, L (2014) 'Fiduciary Relationships: Ensuring the Loyal Exercise of Judgement on Behalf of Another' 130 *Law Quarterly Review* 608

Smith, M and Leslie, N (2018) *The Law of Assignment* 3rd edn (Oxford University Press)

Stevens, R (2007) *Torts and Rights* (Oxford University Press)

—— (2009) 'Damages and the Right to Performance: A *Golden Victory* or Not?' in JW Neyers, R Bronaugh and SGA Pitel (eds), *Exploring Contract Law* (Hart Publishing)

—— (2011) 'Contractual Aspects of Debt Financing' in D Prentice and A Reisberg (eds), *Corporate Finance Law in the UK and EU* (Oxford University Press)

—— (2023) *The Laws of Restitution* (Oxford University Press)

Swadling, W (2006) 'Unjust Delivery' in A Burrows and A Rodger (eds), *Mapping the Law: Essays in Memory of Peter Birks* (Oxford University Press)

Tan, CH (2004) 'Undisclosed Principals and Contract' 120 *Law Quarterly Review* 480

—— (2017) *The Law of Agency* 2nd edn (Academy Publishing)

—— (2021) 'Implied Terms in Undisclosed Agency' 84 *Modern Law Review* 532

Tettenborn, A (1998) 'Agents, Business Owners and Estoppel' 57 *Cambridge Law Journal* 274

—— (2002) 'Assignees, Equities and Cross-Claims: Principles and Confusion' *Lloyds Maritime and Commercial Law Quarterly* 485

—— (2010) 'Problems in Assignment Law: Not Yet out of the Wood?' in A Burrows and E Peel (eds), *Contract Formation and Parties* (Oxford University Press)

—— (2018) 'Transfer of Chattels by Non-Owners: Still and Open Problem' 77 *Cambridge Law Journal* 151

Tham, CH (2019) *Understanding the Law of Assignment* (Cambridge University Press)

Thomas, S (2011) 'The Origins of the Factors Acts 1823 and 1825' 32 *Journal of Legal History* 151

Tolhurst, GJ (2002) 'Equitable Assignment of Legal Rights: A Resolution to a Conundrum' 118 *Law Quarterly Review*

—— (2016) *The Assignment of Contractual Rights* (Hart Publishing)

Tolhurst, GJ and Carter, JW (2014) 'Prohibitions on Assignment: A Choice to be Made' 73 *Cambridge Law Journal* 405

Turner, PG (2008) 'Legal Assignment of Rights of Restricted Assignability' *Lloyd's Maritime and Commercial Law Quarterly* 306

Twigg-Flesner, C (2005) 'Examination Prior to Purchase' 121 *Law Quarterly Review* 205

Van Zwieten, K (2018) *Goode on Principles of Corporate Insolvency Law* (Sweet & Maxwell)

Warren, E (1987) 'Bankruptcy Policy' 54 *University of Chicago Review* 775

Watts, P (2015) 'Some Wear and Tear on *Armagas v Mundogas*: the Tension between Having and Wanting in the Law of Agency' *Lloyd's Maritime and Commercial Law Quarterly* 36

—— (2020) 'Agency' in W Day and S Worthington (eds), *Challenging Private Law: Lord Sumption on the Supreme Court* (Hart Publishing)

Winterton, D (2015) *Money Awards in Contract Law* (Hart Publishing)

Wood, P (1989) *English and International Set-Off* (Sweet & Maxwell)

Worthington, S (1996) *Proprietary Interests in Commercial Transactions* (Oxford University Press)

—— (2006) 'Floating Charges: The Use and Abuse of Doctrinal Analysis' in J Getzler and J Payne (eds), *Company Charges: Spectrum and Beyond* (Hart Publishing)

—— (2012) 'Good Faith, Flawed Assets and the Emasculation of the UK Anti-Deprivation Rule' (2012) 75 *Modern Law Review* 112

TABLE OF CASES

OTHER CASES

TABLE OF STATUTES

STATUTES